MYTHOLOGY

NOTES

including

- *Introduction to Mythology*
  - Egyptian Mythology
  - Babylonian Mythology
  - Indian Mythology
  - Greek Mythology
  - Roman Mythology
  - Norse Mythology
- *Review Questions*
- *Genealogical Tables*
- *Recommended Reading*
- *Comprehensive Index*

by
James Weigel, Jr., M.A.
University of California

INCORPORATED
LINCOLN, NEBRASKA 68501

ISBN 0-8220-0865-3

1991 Printing

Cliffs Notes, Inc. Lincoln, Nebraska

CONTENTS

Preface

In writing a concise *Mythology* of seven different cultures, it is not only necessary to choose the stories carefully, it is essential to select the most pertinent details from several variations of a myth. Frequently there are many versions of a legend or myth. And this accounts for discrepancies between what one writer will say and another's telling of the same tale. Any comparison of the various mythology books on the market will show marked divergences, running from the spelling of names to details of events to the shape and emphasis of the myths. It is impossible to achieve uniformity in this field, both practically and theoretically.

Nor is this surprising. People reporting the same event give widely varying versions of it. So multiply this by centuries of oral transmission through eras of cultural stagnation and upheaval and in distinct geographical locales often separated by hundreds of miles. Then multiply these versions by a conversion into literature, where every author has a unique personality and viewpoint. Finally, watch the myths change over a thousand and more years of literary tradition. The confusion is bound to be truly bewildering. It is perhaps lucky for mythographers that so much of classical literature has been lost, for they would never be done sorting it all out. As it is, there is more than enough disorder in this field. Theories are superabundant.

If one were to combine each account of a myth into one story the result would be as chaotic as life itself. The basic function of myth is to order reality into significant patterns. Therefore, we have tried to organize the various stories in this volume into readable and coherent units, while giving the reader important variations when they occur. Where this work differs in details, spelling, or in the form of a story from other books on the subject, it does not mean that anyone is incorrect, for every writer has had to face the awesome task of making selections on the basis of his own judgment.

The principles of choice behind this volume are these: Does a story reveal something important about the culture from which it came? Does it have interest? Does the shape of the story have meaning? Do the details of a story make sense? Are they important? When variants of a story exist, which details contribute the most to the overall effect? Do the contradictory versions also make sense? Which spelling is the easiest for the reader, and the least obtrusive? Are all of these choices consistent with common sense and faithful to the myths themselves? Does the writing style show some of the fascination of the myth? Is it readable?

This book is not simply an introduction to mythology, it is an introduction to the study of various civilizations as these are revealed in their myths and legends. It is intended to get you started on exploring the fabulous realm of the human imagination in history.

Introduction to Mythology

The simplest and most direct way to approach mythology is to look at its subject matter. In the broadest terms myths are traditional stories about gods, kings, and heroes. Myths often relate the creation of the world and sometimes its future destruction as well. They tell how gods created men. They depict the relationships between various gods and between gods and men. They provide a moral code by which to live. And myths treat the lives of heroes who represent the ideals of a society. In short, myths largely deal with the significant aspects of human and superhuman existence.

It is easy to forget this in reading about the many absurd, barbaric, comic, grotesque, or sentimental occurrences in various mythologies. Yet, on the whole, myths have a certain dignity and eloquence precisely because they do grapple with important matters.

Myths are generally stories that have been handed down for generations, popular tales that embody a collective knowledge. While some may have originated with shamans, priests, or poets, myths belong to a primitive or pre-scientific people as their cultural heritage. Usually they have been shaped by the folk imagination.

Very often myths are accepted as the literal truth. They are not presented as engaging fictions but as fact. Even in the sophisticated, intelligent culture of classical Greece myths were frequently viewed as actualities. And when they were regarded skeptically writers reshaped them to make them more probable and humane.

Forget for the moment that the myths of other cultures are considerably more bizarre and savage. It must seem incredible to us, conditioned as we are by materialism and scientific rationality, that the ancient Greeks for the most part could take seriously a philandering deity like Zeus, an incredible hero like Perseus, or a monster like the Medusa. It would seem to presuppose much ignorance and gullibility. However, the primary appeal of myth is to the imagination, to man's intuitive faculty. In a society where reason is poorly developed or nonexistent, the imagination is the only arbiter of truth. And even where reason is predominant, as it was in classical Greece, the imagination still exerts a strong hold on one's beliefs. A culture, after all, can never abandon its age-old traditions without undergoing disintegration.

In their vital stage, when they are accepted as truth, myths represent the learning of a society, its accumulated knowledge and wisdom. Any body of myths tries to give a comprehensive account of the world and of the people to whom it belongs. It does this through narrative, through memorable stories that deal with matters that perplex and intrigue primitive man. The crude mythology of an Australian tribe; the priestly mythologies of Egypt, Babylonia, and India; the liberating mythology of Greece and Rome; and the heroic mythology of Scandinavia—all offer a way of apprehending reality, of making sense of nature and human life, no matter how irrational they might appear to us. Every mythology has its obscurities, inconsistencies, and absurdities, but the crucial point is that myths attempt to give form to the cosmos and meaning to human life. We shall see this ordering impulse in each of the mythologies in this volume.

Most modern scholars divide the subject into three principal categories: pure myth, heroic saga, and the folk tale. Pure myth is both primitive science and primitive religion. It consists of stories that explain natural phenomena such as the sun, stars, flowers, storms, volcanoes, and so on, or of stories that show how men should behave toward gods. These myths recount how the world came into being, who the various gods are and what powers they control, how these gods affect the world and men, and the means by which men can propitiate these powers.

Gods can be personified natural agents such as fire, sky, earth, water, and the like. But more often they are beings that use specific areas of nature to effect their purposes, just as men operate machines to produce some end. Gods are often visualized as having human shape, feeling human emotions, and performing human acts, even if they are immortal and infinitely more powerful than men. This renders the cosmos more intelligible than it would be if it were ruled by impersonal, capricious forces that were indifferent to man's welfare. Gods, even at their cruelest, are much preferable to stark chaos. And gods that look and act as human beings do make the world appear more bearable, because they sanctify human beauty and strength by giving them supernatural precedent.

In interpreting nature, myths use analogical reasoning, relating the unfamiliar to the familiar by means of likeness. Thus, things in heaven happen the same way they do here on earth. Why does the sun move across the sky? Because some deity is pushing it, riding it, or sailing it through the universe each day. And just as beasts and men beget progeny by copulation, so the primordial elements of nature procreate on each other in most mythologies. Or to give another example, the ancient Greeks must have wondered why the constellations of Ursa Major and Ursa Minor never set below the horizon, whereas other groups of stars did. The mythological solution, related by Ovid in his tale of Callisto, is that they were outcasts. Hera hated those stars and ordered the sea never to let them sink, since they were once the living mistress and son of Hera's mate, Zeus. This shows mythological reasoning and the projection of human feelings onto the natural world.

A coordinate branch of myth deals with the art of getting the gods to effect human purposes. This involves primitive religion with a technological overcast. The gods, having some human qualities, may respond to worship, ritual, supplication, and sacrifice. They are never obliged to help human beings, but they can if they so desire. Gods sometimes show partiality by rewarding a few mortals with good fortune. But generally nature is incalculable. One can never tell where lightning will strike, storms sink ships, wars and plagues ravage, earthquakes wreck cities, or flood, drought, and hail ruin crops. Yet psychologically a man is never totally impotent if he has gods to whom he can appeal. Myths frequently deal with the tributes one should pay a god, the chief of which is piety.

Yet there is an older, darker region of myth involving magic. Magic is also an attempt to influence the gods to fulfill human wishes. The Greeks pretty much expurgated or transmuted this element in their myths, but it has a fairly sizable place in the myths of primitive peoples and in the ancient Near Eastern and

European mythologies. Magic seeks to influence nature by imitation, by mimicking the results one wants. It depends upon analogical thought, whereby like produces like. The savage rite of human sacrifice was supposed to guarantee a plentiful harvest in neolithic societies, because the sprinkling of human blood on the ground would bring the necessary rain to the crops.

In ancient cults throughout the Near East and Europe magic was associated with the worship of the triple-goddess, usually in agricultural communities presided over by a matriarchal queen. The triple-goddess stood for the three phases of the moon—waxing, full, and waning; the three phases of nature—planting, harvest, and winter; and the three phases of womanhood—virgin, mature woman, and crone. In her earthly incarnation as queen she often took a male lover each year, and when his period was through he was ritually murdered. Traces of this archaic religion can be found in Greek mythology, but the Greeks with their patriarchal worship of Zeus managed to suppress it fairly thoroughly.

While men might use religious ritual or magic to induce the gods to grant their requests, it was extremely dangerous to antagonize a supernatural force. The gods were invariably ruthless in punishing acts of impiety or overweening pride. King Ixion, for attempting to ravish the goddess Hera, was struck dead by Zeus's thunderbolt, lashed to a turning wheel in hell, and bitten eternally by snakes. In the *Gilgamesh* epic the mighty Enkidu contracted a fatal illness for insulting Ishtar, the Babylonian fertility goddess. Dozens of myths vividly portray the folly and dire results of neglecting or provoking the gods. This is equally a matter of morality and of influencing nature.

In addition to explaining natural phenomena as the work of gods and showing how men should relate to these powers, myths can explain other things, such as the source and meaning of some ritual. A sacred rite can be impressive in itself, satisfying man's need for comforting repetition in an all-too-unstable world. But myth adds a spiritual dimension to ritual and gives it supernatural sanction. The story of Demeter and Persephone gave a transcendent significance to the Eleusinian rites. And Hesiod, in his tale of how Prometheus tricked Zeus, gave divine precedent to the fact that men get the hide and meat of a sacrificial animal while the gods get the fat and bones.

Myths can also account for the origin of names, whether of places or peoples. The story of Helle falling off the ram with the golden fleece into the sea explains how the Hellespont got its name. Icarus, of course, fell into the Icarian Sea after flying too close to the sun. The legend of Ion tells of the founder of the Ionian race, who also gave his name to the Ionian Sea. And the tale of Zeus creating a formidable race of men from an ant heap explains how Achilles' warriors, the Myrmidons, got their name, since *myrmex* is the Greek word for ant. Fanciful as they are, these stories made ancient geography and racial inheritance more intelligible to a people whose origins were in the remote and misty past.

Myths always express man's need to be aware of his roots. An important part of any mythology is the genealogy of gods, kings, and heroes. The lordly families of Homeric and post-Homeric Greece traced their ancestry to the legendary heroes of the Trojan War—heroes who in turn traced their ancestry back to the gods. The scrupulous attention paid to genealogical lines in myths all over the world stresses that mythical and legendary figures were not created out of the blue but had distinguished blood lines behind them. Even the gods had parents in the cruder, primal elements of nature. Here again in myth divine processes reflect human processes and interests.

If pure myth is explanatory, the heroic saga is often a primitive version of history. The saga condenses and dramatizes lengthy historical events into epic encounters. When Schliemann excavated and discovered the site of Troy in 1870, he lent some credence to the legend of the Trojan War. Archeological evidence has established that a brilliant civilization flourished around the Aegean Sea from about 1500 to 1260 B.C., and that this Mycenaean culture was destroyed by the Dorian invasions, which threw Greece into the dark ages for four centuries. If the actual Trojan War took place with even half the magnitude that Homer describes, Asia Minor and Mycenaean Greece must have been considerably weakened, preparing the way for the Dorian invasions.

Later Greece saw the fall of Troy as the victory of Hellenism over the barbarian East, but it was hardly a victory if the foregoing is true. Yet peoples may rewrite legends to suit themselves. In fact, legends sometimes serve as propaganda to support an existing social structure, as the tale of Theseus was used by Euripides to bolster the faltering Athenian democracy in the Peloponnesian War. A legend is not infrequently a political tool to give added weight to some faction.

And here we come to the most important function of heroic saga—that of establishing a grand past for a people and setting forth the values by which a race is to live. Heroic legends embody the values of a society and orient the individual toward the standards and goals of his culture. They show what manhood consists of and how a great man lives and dies. In doing so they give meaning and direction to life.

Let's look at some of the heroes in this volume to see what values they represent. In general, there are those that fight beasts, those that fight other men, and those that fight forces within themselves. However, men who war with the gods are not heroes at all but evildoers and mountebanks who are properly punished. A hero is inconceivable without conflict and some enemy to overcome.

The most primitive kind of hero is the monster slayer. Beowulf is the perfect example, killing an ogre, an ogress, and a dragon, each of whom threatens the small human settlements of the frozen North. This type clears the earth of ghastly menaces and makes it safe for human habitation. Heracles is a more advanced type, since he not only kills monsters but captures wild beasts as well, preparing the way for animal domestication. Fittingly, Heracles has many offspring, populating the world he has rendered safe.

Of the warrior heroes there is the pure type like Achilles and the Norse heroes. This type fights for personal glory and fame, never mind what the cause of the war may be. Such a hero has no fear of death, lives by a rigid code of honor, and is permeated with the feeling that life is worthless but very delicious. A warrior like this lives to die in battle, winning renown for generations.

Then there is the warrior hero who fights for a dying but illumined culture, and one he knows is doomed. The Homeric hero Hector fights for Troy and for his family, but these responsibilities tend to encumber him when he finally meets Achilles, who has nothing to lose by dying and who is completely dedicated to killing. And King Arthur, after all the splendors of Camelot, is fatally wounded in battle by his illegitimate son, Modred.

There is also the warrior who seeks to establish a kingship or build a city. Aeneas is the exemplar of this type, fighting for a new and coming civilization with the force of destiny in his breast. He represents the values that made Rome triumphant for centuries, even though he is a literary rather than a mythical personage.

Finally we have the metaphysical hero, who sets out on a strange quest. Gilgamesh in his journey to overcome death is such a hero, and his failure carries the sadness of human mortality. But the pure metaphysical hero is Buddha, who conquers within himself all the urges that prevent enlightenment.

Thus we see the spectrum of values and heroic codes that a society can use to shape a civilization. Epic legends show the direction of a culture and what it is likely to accomplish. Legends are not mere entertainments; they serve to educate and channel the energies of the young. Puberty rites in primitive cultures involve rigorous instruction in myth and legend. The boys of classical Greece were expected to memorize large parts of Homer and Hesiod. As Werner Jaeger points out in *Paideia,* the *Iliad* had a profound effect on the spectacular brilliance of Greek civilization. The Achillean thirst for glory helped promote a striving for excellence in every field, which created the stunning geniuses of the Classical Age. Essentially heroic legends are the stuff for which civilizations live and die.

Besides the pure myth and the saga there is another type of story common in primitive cultures: the folk tale or fairy tale. This is a story told for sheer pleasure without any pretense to being factual. The travelers' tales, such as the adventures of Odysseus, are stories of this kind. And the legend of Perseus has a large element of fairy tale and magic. Yet because folk tales are told for pleasure does not mean they cannot have meaning or beauty. The writings of Jung and other psychoanalysts dissuade us from lightly dismissing folk tales as nonsense. They may be a primitive form of fiction, but for that very reason they are close to the tap root of man's imagination. Apuleius' tale of Cupid and Psyche is a delightful literary adaptation of the fairy tale, expressing the hard discipline of the soul before it can recover its true place as the mate of love.

In a sophisticated society myths may be conscious and symbolic creations designed to embody an abstract idea. A story, after all, is far more memorable than a sermon or a treatise. It can present a complicated concept and make it shimmer with implications. Aesop's fables, Plato's philosophical myths, and India's mythical allegories are such stories. As Jesus realized, if one wants to make an abstract idea understandable to the masses one should present it as a story or parable. The tale of the Good Samaritan, for example, shows the broad idea of universal brotherhood very simply. Myths connected with the mystery cults of ancient Greece, such as those of Persephone, Dionysus, and Orpheus, where the hero or heroine enters the kingdom of death to re-emerge later, point not merely to the annual dying and rebirth of vegetation but also to a belief in the immortality of the soul. The fable, the parable, and the allegory all require considerable intelligence to create them and are usually not the product of the popular or folk imagination.

There is yet another type of story often classified as myth that is the result of a conscious literary effort and which belongs to a highly developed culture. This is the romance, the love story in which the hero is dedicated to the pursuit or happiness of a woman. In the realm of heroic action women were almost incidental to the hero's destiny. A woman could help or hinder the hero but his deeds belonged to him alone. Heroes like Heracles, Jason, Theseus, Odysseus, and Aeneas might have romantic entanglements, but they always left the women behind to follow their true calling. In the romance, however, the hero devotes himself to love. Here one sees tales like those of Venus and Adonis, Pyramus and Thisbe, Launcelot and Guinevere, and many more. These tales crop up when a culture begins to grow soft, as in Hellenized Greece, late Augustan Rome and after, or the courtly societies of the late Middle Ages. In Ovid, for instance, the elegant Augustan poet, there is an obsessive preoccupation with love and feminine psychology. It would seem that when a culture lacks monsters to kill, civilizations worth fighting for, or ideas to advance, men seem to dissolve in effeminate idleness, making the art of love their main profession.

Having delineated the major types of stories usually classed as myth—the explanatory myth, the heroic saga, the folk tale, the symbolic story, and the romance—it must be said that these stories are rarely found in their pure form, but are blended and take on multiple functions. Myths have their source in the imagination and can satisfy those needs that require an imaginative solution. Stories are indeed the most impressive records of human life. Many of the myths in this volume have lasted for thousands of years, remaining as fresh as when they were first written down, while the architecture of the age lies buried in ruins. This is because myths have their origin in man's creative faculty, which is vital and permanent.

But why study these old tales? What do they have to offer today's student?

For one thing, in their written form myths are often magnificent literature. Homer, Aeschylus, Sophocles, Euripides, Aristophanes, Plato, and Vergil are among the foremost literary geniuses of all time. Yet even lesser authors and works like *Gilgamesh,* the Indian classics, Pindar, Horace, Ovid, Apuleius, *Beowulf,* the *Eddas,* and Malory make enjoyable reading.

For another, classical mythology formed the basis of a humanistic education throughout the ancient world and from the late Middle Ages down to the twentieth century. Writers from Chaucer to Robert Graves have been steeped in these old myths, so that their works can scarcely be appreciated without some knowledge of them. Furthermore, the art, sculpture, and architecture of the ancient world abounds in mythological themes; and the art and sculpture from the Renaissance to Picasso cannot be fully grasped without an understanding of mythology. Other fields, too, borrow some of their terminology from myths—fields as diverse as psychology, botany, astronomy, and space technology.

The anthropologist and the archeologist study the myths of a people as a means of grasping the culture.

But beyond these advantages a sympathetic reading of the myths of other peoples and ages can keep us from becoming provincial in outlook, locked in the narrow worlds of our own immediate concerns. Myths can show us the marvels that existed long before scientific reasoning shed its progressive light on our perceptions.

Egyptian Mythology

INTRODUCTION

Egyptian religion had ancient origins and lasted for at least 3,500 years. The Egyptians saw divinity in everything—in river, desert, and vegetation; in the sun, moon, and stars; in animals and kings; in birth and death. They created a vast and confusing multitude of gods.

There are literally hundreds of deities, some having animal form, some depicted with human bodies and animal heads, and some of human form. A god like Ra had dozens of names, and often gods had two or more shapes apiece. Political and priestly pressures sometimes brought in new gods and swept the old ones aside. Furthermore, Egyptian religion was local, with different religious centers having different gods and cosmogonies. After listing a few of the major gods, we will give the account of the creation according to the priests at Heliopolis.

Of myths proper there is only one of which we have a complete account—the story of Osiris. The Egyptians took their myths for granted, passing them down by word of mouth without ever fully recording them. The reason we have the myth of Osiris is that Plutarch, the Greco-Roman historian wrote it down.

SOME PRINCIPAL GODS

Ra was the great sun god at Heliopolis. A child in the early morning, a man in his prime at noon, and an old man in the evenings Ra journeyed through the underworld at night to be reborn at dawn. His head was crowned with a solar disk upon which rested the sacred asp, destroyer of the god's enemies.

Shu and ***Tefnut,*** were Ra's children. Shu, the god of air, held up the sky and was represented with an ostrich feather on his head. His sister and wife, Tefnut, was a goddess of dew and rain. She was represented as a lioness or as a woman with the head of a lioness.

Geb and ***Nut*** were the offspring of Shu and Tefnut. Geb was the god of earth, while Nut was the sky goddess. Geb was usually shown as a prostrate man, and Nut arched over him as a woman or a cow. They were separated by their father, Shu.

Osiris was the first child of Geb and Nut, a god of nature and vegetation but also the judge of the dead in the underworld. He was instrumental in civilizing the world, yet was murdered by his envious brother, Set. Osiris was shown as a man in mummy wrappings, crowned with a miter and two ostrich feathers.

Isis, a daughter of Geb and Nut, was the faithful wife of Osiris and a beneficent sorceress. She enjoyed a large cult in antiquity and was represented with a throne on her head.

Set was Osiris' evil brother, the incarnation of wickedness and sterility. He was depicted with a beastly head and tail.

Nephthys was Set's sister and consort, but she loved Osiris and, through cunning, had a child by him. She wore a basket on her head.

Horus, the falcon-headed son of Osiris and Isis, was dedicated to avenging his father's murder.

Anubis, the jackal-headed son of Osiris and Nephthys, prepared the dead and ushered them into the underworld.

Thoth was the god of learning, a benefactor to gods and men. He was the sacred scribe and was shown as a man with an ibis head.

Hathor, the goddess of joy and love, protected women. She was represented as a cow.

Amon, king of the gods, was a patron of the Pharaohs and a god of fertility. He had a plumed crown and was shown with either a ram's head or a human one.

Aten was the monotheistic god presented by the reforming Pharaoh Akhenaton. He was represented simply by a solar disk with rays.

Khepri, the scarab beetle god, rolled the sun before him through the sky and symbolized the ideas of rebirth and eternal life.

Maat, the goddess of truth and justice, was represented as a woman sitting on her heels or standing and wearing an ostrich plume.

The ***Pharaoh,*** or king of Egypt, was worshiped as a god and was believed to have descended from gods.

Sacred animals who were worshiped as gods include ***Apis,*** the bull; ***Petesuchos,*** the crocodile; ***Ba Neb Djedet,*** the sacred ram; and ***Bennu,*** the bird. But many other animals were regarded as holy, including cats and dogs.

THE CREATION

At first there was nothing but ***Nun,*** the primal ocean of chaos which contained the seeds of everything to come. In this jumble of waters the sun god reposed. Finally, by an exertion of will, he emerged from chaos as Ra and gave birth to Shu and Tefnut by himself. In turn Shu, the god of air, and Tefnut, the goddess of moisture, gave birth to Geb and Nut, the earth god and sky goddess. Thus the physical universe was created.

Men were created from Ra's tears. Eons passed and Ra grew decrepit, so the ungrateful race of men plotted against Ra. When Ra learned of these plots he angrily called a council of the gods. The gods decided that mankind must be destroyed, and Ra despatched the goddess Hathor to wipe out humankind. Hathor did an effective job of it, killing men by the tens of thousands until only a tiny remnant was left. Then Ra relented, and men were spared. But Ra was thoroughly sick of the world and retreated into the heavens, leaving Shu to reign in his place. At that time the present world was established.

Against the orders of Ra, Geb, the earth god, and Nut, the sky goddess, married. Then Ra in his wrath ordered Shu, the air god, to separate them. Shu defeated Geb and raised Nut aloft, separating them permanently. However, Nut was pregnant, and Ra had decreed that she could not give birth in any month of any year. Seeing her plight, the god of learning, Thoth, gambled with the moon for extra light and thus was able to add five extra days to the official Egyptian calendar of 360 days. On those five days Nut gave birth to Osiris, Horus the Elder, Set, Isis, and Nepthys, successively. Osiris became the incarnation of good, while Set became the embodiment of evil. In this manner the two poles of morality were fixed once and for all.

OSIRIS

The first son of Geb and Nut, Osiris was tall, slender, and handsome, with jet black hair. When his father, Geb, gave up the reigning power over Egypt and retired into the heavens, Osiris took over the kingship and married his sister, the beautiful Isis. Under his wise authority the Egyptians were persuaded to renounce cannibalism. He taught them farming and the pleasures of music, and he framed a just legal code for them. Egypt flourished peacefully under his rule.

Then Osiris went off to civilize the rest of the world and brought the same blessings to Europe, the Near East, and the Orient. In his absence Isis reigned as queen of Egypt and the land continued to prosper.

However, Osiris had an ugly and evil brother with red, coarse hair like an ass's pelt. This was Set, a born plotter who envied the power and attractiveness of his elder brother. Set had another reason for hating Osiris, since his own wife, Nephthys, had conceived a child by Osiris—the jackal-headed Anubis. By bribery and cunning Set gained many allies during Osiris' absence, and together they devised a plan for the king's death.

When it was announced that Osiris would return, Set held a banquet and invited his brother. After the festivities Set had a beautiful chest brought forth and said that it would belong to the person who fitted it perfectly. After everyone had tried, Osiris stepped into the chest. Then Set and his toadies slammed the lid shut and sealed the joints with lead. Osiris suffocated, the chest was thrown into the Nile, and Set became king of Egypt.

When Isis learned of her husband's death she traveled along the Nile in the deepest grief, searching for the chest containing Osiris. She found Anubis, who had been abandoned by

Nephthys, and she nursed and educated him. Isis continued looking for Osiris through repeated discouragements, until one day she learned the chest had sailed to Phoenicia, where a tamarisk tree had enveloped it within its trunk.

Isis went to Phoenicia and found the tree in the king's palace serving as a pillar. Isis taught the court ladies the art of perfumery and hair dressing, and upon meeting the queen Ishtar, she was engaged as a nurse to Ishtar's infant son. At night she performed a magic ritual to make the infant immortal by burning away his mortal parts, but Ishtar interrupted the ceremony and the spell was broken. Then Isis revealed herself as a goddess in all her glory and asked to have the chest in the palace pillar. Awed, Ishtar granted the request, and Isis returned to Egypt with the chest.

Aided by Nephthys, Isis revived Osiris through magic and conceived a son by him. And Set then put her in prison, from which she escaped with the help of Anubis. Isis fled to the swamps of the Nile delta and, living like a peasant, she gave birth to Osiris' son, Horus the hawk, born to avenge his father's murder.

In fear of Set, Isis raised Horus in seclusion. The boy was bitten by beasts, stung by a scorpion, and suffered intense pains throughout his childhood, and only his mother's witchcraft managed to save him. Often Osiris would appear to the young Horus to instruct him in the arts of war in preparation for the coming battle with Set. Horus grew to manhood as a valiant, handsome young general.

In time Set learned of Horus' existence and of his destiny to take over the throne of Egypt. Set also learned that Isis possessed the chest containing Osiris' corpse, so at night Set would hunt through the Nile delta in search of the chest. At length he found it and cut Osiris' body into fourteen pieces and threw them into the Nile.

Isis was appalled at this second calamity to befall her husband, but with her customary patience she collected thirteen pieces of Osiris' body from the river. Horus, having learned the art of sorcery, was able to join his father's body together again. However, Osiris' genitals had been eaten by some fish, so Isis was obliged to make a model of them.

By this time Horus had gathered an army with which to attack Set. Under Set's reign Egypt had become parched and infertile, and many of Set's followers were deserting to serve Horus. After restoring his father's body, Horus set out to wreak vengeance on the dreadful king. Set and Horus fought furiously for three days and nights in hand-to-hand combat, and Set was defeated. Horus turned the wretched captive over to his mother Isis and went off to pursue and kill Set's followers.

Set seemed merely pitiable in chains, and using all his powers of persuasion, he talked the forgiving Isis into releasing him. When Horus returned and learned of this, his anger was so great that he chopped off his mother's head. The god Thoth then replaced Isis' head with that of the cow-goddess Hathor and brought her back to life.

Together Horus and Isis pursued Set, and when they met the fighting was even more intense. Set managed to grab Horus' eye and tear it out, but Horus wrested it back and finally drove Set into the Red Sea forever.

Horus and Isis then returned to the temple where Osiris' body lay. Horus embraced the body and fed it his own eye that had been torn out, and Osiris revived as a truly godlike personage. Next Horus prepared a ladder for his father to ascend into heaven. By this means Osiris rose into the sky, with Isis on one side of him and Nephthys on the other. The gods sat in judgment on him, and with Thoth as his advocate Osiris was declared to have lived a pure and truthful life. From there Osiris went to the Seat of Judgment, where he in turn was allowed to judge the souls of the dead.

Horus was recognized by the gods as being Osiris' legitimate son and the rightful heir to the throne of Egypt. Under his dominion Egypt grew fruitful again, and he sired four pure sons from whom the entire line of Egyptian Pharaohs descended.

Commentary

In some interpretations of the myth of Osiris the main figures of the myth sumbolize the physical features of Egypt itself. Thus, Osiris represents the Nile with its annual flooding and withdrawal; Isis represents the fertile farm land of Egypt, which was made fecund by the Nile; Set represents the arid desert that separates the Nile and the fertile land; while Nephthys stands for the marginal areas between the farm land and desert. This naturalistic approach may stem from the fact that the lineage of these gods symbolized forces of nature—earth, sky, air, moisture, the sun.

Yet the main features of the myth are largely moral, depicting the eternal struggle between the powers of good and evil. Osiris is fearless, self-sacrificing, gentle, in harmony with himself, a benefactor to mankind; whereas Set is fearful, devious, full of envy and hate, sterile, never at peace. Osiris commands undying loyalty, while Set is deserted when his luck wears thin. The gods aid Osiris' family through hardships, but Set has merely his own strength to rely on. Lastly, goodness leads to one's resurrection and an honored place in the afterworld, but evil leads only to a despised exile.

One point worth remarking about some Egyptian gods, such as Ra, Shu, and Geb, is that they suffer the same vicissitudes as earthly monarchs. They reign for a while in Egypt, their power begins to dwindle, and they retire into the sky, leaving their kingdom to a son. Moreover, Osiris has a mortal body and dies like any man. And he must be restored to life through magic and love. One can link this to the annual death and rebirth of vegetation, but it has more to do with the idea of the soul's immortality and a regeneration beyond the grave.

Babylonian Mythology

INTRODUCTION

Most records of Babylonian myths date from 700 B.C., when they were transcribed in cuneiform on clay tablets and stored in the library of the Assyrian King Ashurbanipal at Nineveh. However, the two major Babylonian epics probably originated around 2000 B.C.. The *Epic of Creation* justifies Marduk's rule over gods and men; and it reflects the political supremacy of Babylon in Mesopotamia, since Marduk was the chief god of that city. The *Gilgamesh Epic* shows the failure of man's quest to overcome death.

Generally Babylonian mythology lacks the transcendental quality of the myth of Osiris. It is more earth-bound and more materialistic. Death puts an end to the sensual pleasures of life, and the underworld of the dead is the most dismal place imaginable. The Babylonian gods themselves indulge in eroticism, feasting, and fighting. But if the values are coarser and more masculine, the Babylonians produced a literary triumph in the *Gilgamesh Epic*.

THE MAJOR GODS

Anu, the head of the gods, reigned in the uppermost part of heaven and had an army of stars to destroy evildoers.

Enlil, god of the hurricane and deluge, was also the source of royal power and dealt out good and evil to men.

Ea, a god of the waters, was a benefactor to nature and men by virtue of his all-encompassing wisdom.

Marduk was a fertility god and the principal deity of Babylon. He established lordship over all the other gods by killing the malevolent and chaotic Tiamat and by creating the world out of Tiamat's body.

Sin, the moon god, was an enemy to the wicked, shining his nightly light upon their deeds. His children were Shamash, the sun, and Ishtar, the planet Venus.

Shamash was the sun god, a dispenser of light and justice to the world, but also the god of prophecy.

Ishtar, one of the most popular Babylonian deities, was the goddess of sexuality, a potent force among beasts and men. She sanctified temple prostitution. Lustful herself, Ishtar had numerous lovers, most of whom had dreadful fates.

One of Ishtar's lovers was the harvest god ***Tammuz.*** When he died of her love Ishtar wailed bitterly. Thinking to retrieve Tammuz from the kingdom of death, Ishtar entered the seven portals to the underworld. At each portal she left one of her garments or pieces of jewelry until at last she stood naked before Ereshkigal, the queen of the dead. Ereshkigal had Ishtar imprisoned and assaulted her with sixty illnesses. During this incarceration the earth withered and became desolate, and the gods of heaven mourned. Finally Ea, the god of wisdom, took matters in hand and through his magical intervention Ishtar was released. Allowed to leave, she gathered up her garments and jewelry, accompanied by Tammuz, who was allowed to stand guard at the gates of heaven. Upon Ishtar's return the earth changed from winter to spring.

THE CREATION

Everything originated with water. From the mixture of sweet water, Apsu, with salt water, Tiamat, the gods arose. Apsu and Tiamat gave birth to Mummu, the tumult of the waves, and to Lakhmu and Lakhamu, a pair of gigantic serpents. In turn these serpents produced Anshar, the heavens, and Kishar, the earthly world. And from these two came the great gods, Anu, Enlil, and Ea, as well as the other gods of the sky, earth, and the underworld.

Many of these new gods were noisy, which upset Apsu and Tiamat, since they could not rest. These primordial goddesses then discussed whether they should annihilate their progeny.

When Ea, the all-knowing, learned of Apsu's plan to destroy the gods he used his magic to capture her and Mummu. Tiamat was furious and created a monstrous army of gods and freak creatures to punish Ea and his cohorts.

Ea went to his father Anshar, and Anshar advised him to send Anu to fight Tiamat. But both Anu and Ea were afraid of the goddess and her army. Then Ea called Marduk forth. Marduk promised to conquer Tiamat if he were given supreme authority over the gods. The gods agreed that he was to have lordship and feasted in his honor. Marduk was invested with the scepter, the throne, and an invincible weapon.

Armed with bow and arrows, lightning, the winds, a hurricane, and a special net, Marduk rode forth to meet Tiamat in his chariot, which was a tempest, drawn by four fearsome steeds. They clashed and Marduk caught Tiamat in his net. When she opened her mouth to swallow him, Marduk let loose the hurricane, which filled her jaws and belly, thereby stunning her. Then Marduk shot an arrow into her belly and killed her. Tiamat's army fled in confusion at her downfall, but Marduk caught them in his net, chained them, and cast them into the underworld.

As he was cutting up Tiamat's body, Marduk conceived a plan. From one half of her body he made the dome of the heavens, and with the other half he made the earth. He established the dwelling of the gods, fixed the positions of the stars, ordered the movements of the heavenly bodies, and set the length of the year. Then to gladden the hearts of the gods Marduk created men from the blood of Kingu, the general of Tiamat's army. Finally, he made rivers, vegetation, and animals, which completed the creation. In recognition of his triumphs the gods bestowed all of their titles and powers on Marduk, making him the God of Gods.

THE FLOOD

Apparently the gods were displeased with the human race, for they held a council in which it was agreed that mankind should be drowned. But Ea, the god of wisdom, wished to spare human beings. So Ea told one man, Uta-Napishtim, to build a ship for his family and all living creatures. Uta-Napishtim worked diligently, and by the time the rains came his ship was prepared. For six days and nights a foul rain flooded everything on earth, and even the gods became fearful. By the seventh day the winds and rains ceased. All but Uta-Napishtim and his family had become mud. The ship came to rest upon Mount Nisir, and Uta-Napishtim sent forth birds to find out whether the waters had subsided enough to disembark. When a raven failed to return Uta-Napishtim left the ship and offered a sacrifice to the gods on the mountain peak. Only Enlil, god of the tempest, was angered to see that humanity had been spared. But Ea managed to placate Enlil with soft words, and in token of his reconciliation Enlil gave Uta-Napishtim and his wife the gift of immortality.

GILGAMESH

Over the ancient Sumerian city of Uruk there once ruled a wise and powerful but tyrannical king named Gilgamesh. He was two-thirds a god and one-third a mortal, famed for his exploits in war and for his prowess as an unbeatable wrestler. Gilgamesh was also lustful and he would abduct any woman who took his fancy whether she was single or married. The people of Uruk were greatly distressed at this, for no one could overcome Gilgamesh. So they prayed to the goddess Aruru to fashion a man who could overpower Gilgamesh in order that he would leave their women in peace.

Aruru then created the mighty Enkidu, a hairy man with legs like a bull. Enkidu roamed with the wild beasts and enabled them to escape the traps of hunters. On hearing of Enkidu's strength, Gilgamesh sent a courtesan out to Enkidu's watering place to entice him. When she saw Enkidu the courtesan disrobed, exposing her breasts, and Enkidu went to lie with her. After this his animal companions shunned him because Enkidu had lost his natural innocence. Enkidu then had nothing to do but follow the courtesan's advice and return with her to Uruk.

Back in his palace Gilgamesh dreamed of struggling with a powerful man who could master him. When he told the dream to his mother, Ninsun, she said it meant that he and Enkidu would become close companions. And after an awesome wrestling match Gilgamesh and Enkidu sat down together as friends. Enkidu was invited to live in the palace and share the honors with Gilgamesh.

One night Enkidu had a nightmare in which he was snatched up by a strange, terrible creature with eagle claws who cast him into the underworld of death. When Gilgamesh heard of the dream he offered a sacrifice to Shamash, the sun god, who advised him to go and fight Khumbaba the Strong, the king of the Cedar Mountain. When they learned of his plan to go to the Cedar Mountain, Enkidu, Ninsun, and the people of Uruk tried to dissuade Gilgamesh, to no avail. Gilgamesh was determined to make the long, arduous journey and battle Khumbaba, so Enkidu joined his friend and the two set forth.

They traveled northwest, leaving their fertile land behind, crossing a vast desert, reaching the Amanus Mountains, and finally arriving at the resplendent Cedar Mountain and the stockade of the monster Khumbaba. Enkidu's heart quailed within him, but Gilgamesh issued a challenge to Khumbaba. No answer came, so they made a sacrifice to the gods and settled down for the night. During the night Gilgamesh had a dream of victory. In the morning Khumbaba charged them, and after a terrific fight Gilgamesh was able to knock Khumbaba to the ground, where Enkidu cut his head off. With the monster dead, Gilgamesh was able to cut down the sacred cedars for the temples of Uruk.

The two heroes bathed, dressed, and made offerings to the gods. Then Ishtar appeared to Gilgamesh and tried to seduce him, but he spurned her, saying that her lovers usually had dire fates. When Gilgamesh and Enkidu returned to Uruk with the cedars Ishtar had her vengeance planned. With the help of Anu she loosed the Bull of Heaven against Uruk. In the course of wrecking the city the bull was caught and slaughtered by Gilgamesh and Enkidu. Then in an act of utter rashness Enkidu threw the bull's hide in Ishtar's face, telling her he'd do the same to her if he could. The goddess Ishtar then laid a mortal curse upon Enkidu and after twelve days of sickness he died.

Gilgamesh was inconsolable over the death of his friend, for he realized that he must die one day as well. Determined to find the secret of immortality, Gilgamesh went forth in search of Uta-Napishtim, the man on whom Enlil had conferred life everlasting. He traveled west to the far-off Mount Mashu, which was guarded by Scorpion-Men. With a trembling heart Gilgamesh approached the chief Scorpion-Man, who permitted him passage into the mountain. After a long time in a tunnel he stepped out into the garden of a goddess. The goddess advised Gilgamesh to return home, enjoy life, and accept death gracefully; but Gilgamesh was insistent on finding Uta-Napishtim, so the goddess directed him to Uta-Napishtim's boatman. The boatman warned of the turbulent waters of death that surrounded Uta-Napishtim's dwelling. However, Gilgamesh would not be put off, and with the boatman's help he managed to cross the perilous waters. At last Gilgamesh arrived at the home of the immortal man.

When Gilgamesh told Uta-Napishtim of his quest for eternal life, Uta-Napishtim laughed at his foolishness and told his own story of how he had won immortality. Then Uta-Napishtim challenged Gilgamesh to stay awake, as he himself had done, for six days and seven nights. But the exhausted Gilgamesh had already fallen asleep.

The wife of Uta-Napishtim took pity on the sleeping hero and persuaded her husband to reveal the secret of immortality. They awoke Gilgamesh and told him of a prickly plant that lay at the bottom of the sea. Gilgamesh set off at once to find the plant, and when he came to the ocean edge he tied boulders to his feet and plunged in. He sank to the bottom, found and plucked the prickly plant, untied the boulders and swam to the surface with the precious plant. Gilgamesh went homeward with a high heart, for now he could confer everlasting life on himself and the people of Uruk. He crossed the waters of death, the garden of the goddess; he went through Mount Mashu and traveled eastward.

Within a few day's journey of home Gilgamesh laid the plant on a rock and dove into a small lake to bathe. And while he was swimming a snake approached the plant and ate it. Gilgamesh wept long and bitterly to think he had wasted his enormous effort to gain eternal life. The snakes would live forever, but human beings must die. Gilgamesh returned to Uruk with a broken heart. He knew what a miserable existence the dead lived in the netherworld, for Enkidu had revealed it to him. His only consolation was that the walls of Uruk would outlast him as monuments to Gilgamesh's reign.

Commentary

Babylonian myths appear more dynamic and masculine than those of Egypt. The prominent gods are male except for Ishtar. In the creation myth it is the male Marduk who slays the monster-goddess Tiamat and orders the cosmos. And Uta-Napishtim is a patriarch much like the biblical Noah. But beyond this Gilgamesh is a more imposing figure than Osiris. Isis is the dominant figure of the myth of Osiris, but Gilgamesh towers over others in his own legend. Whereas Osiris is idealized and static, Gilgamesh is drawn as a real man capable of development. If Gilgamesh is lecherous and headstrong, he is also manly, courageous, a true friend, a superb fighter, and a king who tries to give his people immortality. He suffers as we do, and he is obliged to face death as each of us must.

Furthermore, Gilgamesh grows in maturity as the story progresses. At first he's a self-centered despot who cares only for fighting and women. Then he makes a friend of Enkidu and the two of them act partly for the benefit of Uruk in killing the monster Khumbaba, bringing home the cedars and slaying the celestial Bull. Finally, Gilgamesh goes off to procure immortality for himself and his people, sparing himself nothing in the attempt. If his story has many legendary elements we recognize an authentic hero in Gilgamesh.

Indian Mythology

INTRODUCTION

Indian religion and mythology are closely interwoven and cannot really be separated. Moreover, both are so vast and confused that any generalization is likely to oversimplify. The earliest Indian texts are the *Vedas,* a series of sacred hymns in honor of the Aryan gods, who personified natural forces such as the sun, storm, fire, soma, and the like. The Vedic religion was materialistic, devoted to obtaining power, prosperity, health, and other blessings by means of ritual and sacrifice.

By the time of Buddha around 500 B.C., the old Vedic religion had been transformed by Brahmin priests into a fantastical hodgepodge, with the priests claiming godlike powers for themselves. Buddha addressed himself to the problem of human suffering and discovered a way to eliminate it through disciplined living and giving up one's desires. He gained so many followers that the Brahmins were forced to incorporate his ideas into their teachings. The result was Hinduism, a modified polytheism with three major gods: Brahma, Vishnu, and Siva.

We will look at the principal Vedic and Hindu gods and relate two appropriate myths. Then we will view two legends, the first deriving from the *Ramayana* and the second treating the life of Buddha.

THE MAIN VEDIC GODS

Indra is the main god of the *Vedas,* a hard-drinking, swaggering warrior who rides his solar chariot across the sky and wields the thunderbolt. As a storm god he brings the rain to fertilize India's parched soil.

Mitra and ***Varuna*** maintain the cosmic order. ***Mitra,*** the sun, presides over contracts and friendship, while ***Varuna,*** the moon, supervises oaths. Like Indra, these gods reflect the values of the warrior caste.

Agni is the priest's god of fire. He presides at the altar and hearth, exists as lightning, and blazes at the heart of the sun.

Brihaspati is the god of incantation and ritual, the personification of priestly magic.

Soma is both a narcotic plant and a god who gives inspiration, liberates men, and represents the principle of life.

Savitar is the god of motion, and whatever moves or acts is dependent on this deity with golden eyes, hands, and tongues.

Ushas is the beautiful, charming goddess of the dawn, a source of delight to all living creatures.

Puchan brings all things into relationship, blessing marriage, providing food, guiding travelers, and ushering the dead.

Siva is the terrifying god of destruction, a deity so formidable that people must flatter him to avert calamity.

Kali is Siva's wife, a bloodthirsty fertility goddess decorated with emblems of death.

Prajapati is the master of created beings, the father of gods and demons, and the protector of those who procreate.

The ***Devas*** and ***Asuras*** are gods and demons, respectively, and battle each other with magical powers.

The ***Rakshas*** are evil semi-divine creatures that practice black magic and afflict men with misfortune.

INDRA AND THE DRAGON

Once the mighty priest Tvashtri, out of dislike for the god Indra, created a three-headed son to take over Indra's throne. This son was a pious ascetic who appeared to be mastering the universe with his three heads, which made Indra uneasy. After futilely tempting Tvashtri's son with dancing girls, Indra slew the radiant young man with a thunderbolt and ordered that his three heads be cut off.

Enraged, Tvashtri made a colossal dragon named Vritra to destroy Indra. This serpent reached up to the heavens and swallowed Indra. But Indra tickled its throat and leapt out to resume battle. The dragon proved too strong and Indra had to flee. At length he went to the god Vishnu, who advised him to compromise with the dragon. The serpent agreed to peace, provided that Indra did not attack it with solid or liquid, or attack it by day or night. Indra, however, nursed his resentment and tried to get around this agreement.

One evening at twilight Indra saw a huge column of foam containing the god Vishnu, so he hurled this at the dragon, who fell dead. The gods and men rejoiced at the serpent's death, but Indra bore a great sin for killing a priest's son.

HINDU GODS AND CONCEPTS

Brahma refers to the spiritual reality underlying all phenomena, and is sometimes personified as a god. Brahma emerged from the golden egg created by the waters of chaos and established every universe.

Maya is the veil of illusion, the sensuous appearances that delude human beings into materialism.

The ***Transmigration of Souls*** refers to the propensity of souls to incarnate themselves in various material forms, from the mineral to the superhuman. Since soul matter is indestructible, each soul lives innumerable lives.

Karma refers to the debt of sin incurred in the past and in this present life, a debt that must be paid before the soul is to reach perfection.

Vishnu is the supreme Hindu god. He rests on the cosmic waters between creations, or universes; and in each creation he takes on some avatar or material form such as a fish, a wild boar, a turtle, a lion, a dwarf, a man. His worship is marked by affectionate piety and devotion.

Siva is an extremely important Hindu god, the dancing deity of creation and destruction. He has four arms and has a third eye on his forehead with which he destroys. His worship is marked by asceticism.

Parvati is Siva's wife, a goddess symbolic of his power and ruthless in her battles against demons under her various names and aspects.

Ganesa is the popular god of prosperity, a son of Siva and Parvati with four arms and an elephant's head.

BHRIGU AND THE THREE GODS

Once the wise men of India sent Bhrigu the Wise to find out which god was most worthy of the priests' worship: Brahma, Vishnu, or Siva. Bhrigu approached Brahma and omitted one of the proper forms due the god, so Brahma reproached him, accepted Bhrigu's apologies, and forgave him. Then Bhrigu went to Siva and again neglected to pay the proper respect, at which Siva nearly burned him to a crisp with his third eye. Only the most profuse apologies saved Bhrigu from destruction. Then Bhrigu went to Vishnu's home, where Vishnu lay asleep on the floor. And Bhrigu kicked Vishnu in the chest, whereupon Vishnu awoke, asked him if he'd hurt his foot and then proceeded to massage Bhrigu's foot. Bhrigu then proclaimed Vishnu the greatest god of all because he conquered with generosity and kindness.

Commentary

With the early Vedic gods one sees a large element of nature worship and an attempt to master nature. But even here there is a tendency to philosophical abstraction. In the myth of Indra and the dragon one is in a world where might and cunning predominate, and one in which the power of the priests is enough to threaten the most mighty god, Indra. Myths in which a sky god overpowers a terrible serpent are common, but here a strong admixture of priestly arrogance is evident.

With the Hindu gods and concepts the philosophical strain becomes dominant, and morality exercises more of a role. In the myth of Bhrigu and the three gods, one is in a world where generosity and kindness are more important than reprimands or retaliative force.

RAMA AND SITA

No one surpassed the prince Rama in strength, handsomeness, wisdom, or piety. He won the princess Sita by bending a tremendous bow that others could not even lift. On the day before he was to assume rulership of his father's kingdom, Rama's stepmother, out of jealousy and fear, succeeded in having Rama sent into exile so that her own son might assume the throne. Rama was to enter the most savage jungles and remain there for fourteen years. When Rama tried to persuade the beautiful and gentle Sita to stay at home, Sita insisted that her husband's tribulations were her own, and she would share his exile. Further, one of Rama's brothers, Lakshman, accompanied Rama into the forests to serve his brother.

On their journey the three exiles came across the poet Valmiki, who promised to write a glorious epic about them called the *Ramayana*. They also came upon a holy hermit, who gave Rama a splendid bow and arrow created by the gods. At length Rama, Sita, and Lakshman came to the barbaric southern jungles of India, a place inhabited by the savage magicians called Rakshas. Rama built a home in an open meadow with Lakshman's help.

One day a coarse Raksha maiden fell in love with Rama and wished to murder Sita, but Rama jestingly rejected her advances. In a fury the Raksha girl sprang at Sita to kill her, and only Rama's and Lakshman's quickness prevented her. Lakshman cut off her nose and sent her home howling to her brother Ravan, who was king of the Rakshas. Then Rama and Lakshman had to battle and defeat the two demon-warriors who attended the Raksha princess.

The disfigured girl told Ravan of Sita's beauty and urged him to take revenge. Ravan had a Raksha transformed into a lovely, jeweled deer. When Sita saw this deer she became determined to have it against the warnings of Lakshman and Rama. Finally Rama went hunting for the deer and shot it. As it died it cried out for help in a perfect imitation of Rama's voice. Lakshman knew a trick was involved, but the distraught Sita sent him after Rama. And while she was alone the wicked Ravan came disguised as a hermit and abducted Sita in his flying chariot.

Rama and his brother had no idea of what had happened to the vanished Sita until a vulture told them that Ravan had kidnaped her. The two brothers then came across the monkey-king and his adviser, both of whom had been banished by the monkey-king's monstrous brother. In return for Rama's help in defeating this brother the monkey-king promised Rama aid in finding and recovering Sita. So Rama reestablished the monkey-king on his throne, and monkeys were sent to all parts of India to locate Sita. The bravest monkey of all found her on the island of Ceylon, a lonely prisoner in the palace of Ravan.

Rama vowed to destroy Ravan, and he went to the Ocean determined to obtain passage to Ceylon. After the Ocean was stirred into terrible storms by Rama's arrows, it told Rama to seek the help of the god Nala, an architect who directed the monkeys to build a golden bridge of boulders and trees over to Ceylon. In five days the bridge was built; and Rama, Lakshman, and the army of monkeys crossed it to meet Ravan and his magicians in battle.

The fighting raged for days while Rama's side suffered many losses, but gradually Rama, Lakshman, and the monkeys managed to kill off some fearsome enemies. The terrible battle ended when Rama slew Ravan with his holy arrow.

At this the gods sang Rama's praises, for Rama was the incarnation of Vishnu sent to deliver the world from the kingdom of Rakshas.

When Sita approached Rama before throngs of people Rama ignored his freed wife. In utter despair at Rama's rejection, Sita ordered that her funeral pyre be built, and with a heavy heart she entered the flames. However, the flames did not even singe her, a miraculous proof of Sita's purity during her imprisonment under Ravan. Having satisfied everyone about his wife's loyalty in this manner, Rama embraced Sita, and husband and wife were reunited. Then Rama asked Indra, the thunder-god, to restore the slain monkeys to life, which Indra did. And in the end Rama took Sita back to his father's kingdom and ruled it wisely.

BUDDHA

Queen Maya had a dream at the conception of the future Buddha in which a god entered her womb as a small white elephant and the heavens sang for joy. Wise men interpreted the dream as meaning her son would either be a universal king or a supreme saint. When the Buddha was born he emerged painlessly from his mother's side and performed a ritual by which he mastered the world. Seven days later Queen Maya died of joy and was transported into heaven. The infant was named Siddhartha; his family name was Gautama.

When Siddhartha was twelve his father, the rajah, called a council in which it was decided that the boy must never see human suffering or death if he was to become a universal king. Later, his father urged him to acquire a wife in order to bind him to a life of sensual indulgence. Siddhartha sought out the beautiful Yasodhara, daughter of one of his father's ministers; and he won her through his amazing prowess in riding, fencing, and wrestling. For a while Siddhartha lived a pleasurable life with Yasodhara, insulated from the cares of the world. Then one day he came upon an old man who explained that aging happens to everyone. He pondered the misery of this, and soon came to learn of disease and death. Finally he met a begging ascetic, a humble holy man with peace of mind, and he determined to become a monk as well. Leaving his wife, his newborn son, his palace, and his servants, Siddhartha set out to find the truth about human existence.

In his monastic life he was called Sakyamuni and for a time became a disciple of the Yogis, drifting from hermitage to hermitage. Dissatisifed with Yoga, he underwent a severe self-discipline in which he almost starved himself to death and wrecked his intellect. After six years of this he decided that asceticism was pointless, since it ruined the body and enfeebled the mind. His five disciples were greatly disturbed at his renunciation of harsh self-discipline, but Sakyamuni was persistent in seeking the truth.

He went off through the jungle, his body giving off a wondrous light that attracted birds and animals. He was looking for the sacred tree of wisdom, and when he found this Bodhi tree he sat down under it, determined not to rise until he had solved the problem of human suffering. The demon Mara, the Tempter, sent three voluptuous daughters to seduce Sakyamuni. When they failed, Mara sent an army of devils to assault him, but they too proved ineffective. At last Mara hurled his terrible disk at Sakyamuni to slay him, but the disk was transformed into a wreath of flowers suspended over his head.

As night fell vision upon vision came to Sakyamuni. He saw all his past lives, saw the chain of causation that bound every living being, saw the cause of the endless cycle of birth, suffering, and death, and saw the way to liberation, or Nirvana. By dawn he had reached perfect enlightenment, but he remained a week in meditation and another five weeks in solitude. He found he had a choice between entering Nirvana immediately or of teaching what he had learned for several more years on earth. Against his own reluctance he decided to teach, even though his knowledge was hardly communicable in words, and though very few could truly grasp his knowledge.

Briefly, his discovery was this: Birth, pain, decay, and death through innumerable lives are the result of attachment to the material world. Most souls want to incarnate themselves in matter and enjoy the pleasures to be had. This selfish desire creates a succession of lives and sufferings. In order to free oneself of pain a man must practice non-attachment by surrendering his longings to achieve an encompassing love for all creatures. Only in this manner can the soul attain its true estate of everlasting joy.

Now a Buddha, or Enlightened One, he returned to his five disillusioned disciples and overcame their loathing for him through love. After forty-four years of wandering Buddha gave his first sermon in the Deer Park at Benares. He taught the value of moderation, mental clarity, and universal compassion, as opposed to a life of sensual pleasures or one of self-laceration. By his gentleness, lucidity, and strength of character he converted thousands to his new teachings. His wisdom enabled him to perform miracles.

At the age of eighty, on the point of death, he told his weeping followers they would have his doctrines to comfort them, but they must watch and pray always. His final words were, "Work out your own salvation with diligence." Then he went into meditation, was transfigured with ecstasy, and at last passed into Nirvana.

Commentary

In the legend of Rama and Sita, which was written by Valmiki in the sixth century B.C., the hero is a mixture of types. Rama seems saintly in going into exile, full of consideration for everyone. When Sita is abducted, however, he becomes a great violent warrior determined to annihilate the enemy. Originally a loving husband, he treats Sita badly to prove her virtue. Finally, he returns home to rule as king. In this combination of holy man, warrior, scornful husband, king, and a god's incarnation one sees the diverse aspirations of Indian society transformed into a plausible hero.

The story of Buddha is only partially legendary, but it reveals a man whose steadfast pursuit of the truth led him to one of the most influential revelations in human history. We include it here to show a relatively slight mythical overlay on an actual personality; in contrast to Gilgamesh, an actual Sumerian king whose life is largely legendary; and in contrast to Osiris, where a remote figure has become entirely mythical.

Greek Mythology

INTRODUCTION

Greek myths and legends form the richest, most fertile collection of stories in Western culture, if we exclude the Bible. Yet despite their diversity they tend to share a common outlook on life. The Greeks cherished life and believed in living it to the fullest degree, since death was an inevitable fact. While the mystery cults accepted the idea of a resurrection after death, they were a minority. To Homer death was a dismal state, whereas life itself was dangerous, thrilling, glorious. If the ordinary person was bound to perish, so were the great royal dynasties and the mightiest heroes. But this idea did not sadden the Greeks as it had the Babylonian scribes who wrote of Gilgamesh. The Greeks responded with enthusiasm. They felt the only answer to death that was worthy of a man was to carve an imperishable legend by magnificent deeds. The Greeks pursued fame with astonishing energy in the five centuries from Homer to Alexander the Great. They were a tough, restless, ambitious, hard-living, imaginative race. But their lust for reputation made them touchy about their honor, for they were also feisty and vengeful. Their stories show all of these traits in abundance.

The Olympian gods mirrored these Greek qualities faithfully, being quarrelsome, unforgiving deities who enjoyed warring, banqueting, and fornicating. They were always depicted in human form with beautiful, powerful bodies. Thus they were not only humanly intelligible but extremely pleasing to the eye as well. The Greeks greatly admired strength, beauty, and intelligence. And to them man was the measure of all things.

Few mythologies have produced such a wealth of heroes. This was the natural result of the Greek urge for fame. The heroes tend to be adventurers and fighters—bold, experienced, fierce, strong, and often clever. Their feats were far above those of ordinary humanity. However, they also had serious failings that sometimes ruined them: flaws such as overweening pride, rashness, cruelty, which arose from the very source of their successes—ambition. With Greek heroes ambition was intense, occasionally aspiring to godlike powers. As models of human excellence they provided standards for Greek youths to emulate.

The legends of tragic dynasties show this same ambivalence. Despite their worldly power the royal families of Crete, Mycenae, Thebes, and Athens were afflicted with their own particular faults that rendered them vulnerable to disaster: pride of power, ruthlessness in getting revenge, stubbornness in pursuing some goal, and sexual conflict. No race has understood quite as clearly as the Greeks how character is destiny, or how our very achievements can stem from the same source as crime.

In the tale of the Trojan War the heroic and tragic elements are blended. This is perhaps the finest legend of Greek culture. The chief heroes of this story, Achilles and Hector, were doomed to a premature and violent death, but there was a measure of grandeur in their code of honor and in their defiance of fate. Most of the survivors, too, were doomed or suffered a long ordeal. It was a war which no one would win.

In the end the ancient Greeks achieved the permanent fame they sought so avidly. And their mythology has been a mainstay of Western art and literature for well over two thousand years.

THE TITANS

Gaea (Ge), the earth, and her son ***Uranus***, the heavens, produced the Titans, among other beings. The Titans were the old gods who were supplanted by the Olympian gods. Their mother Gaea was probably a neolithic earth-mother who was pushed into the background by the partriarchal gods of the Indo-Europeans who invaded Greece during the second milennium B.C., but her worship persisted even into the Classical Age.

Cronus was the chief Titan, a ruling deity who obtained his power by castrating his father Uranus. Cronus married his sister Rhea, and together they produced the Olympian gods, whom Cronus swallowed at birth to prevent them from seizing the throne. His son Zeus defeated him and the other Titans and bound them in the underworld. Cronus' Latin name was ***Saturn.***

Rhea was Cronus' wife. Vexed at having him swallow their children, she hid Zeus from him and gave him a stone to swallow instead.

Oceanus was the unending stream that encircled the world, a Titan, who with his wife ***Tethys*** produced the rivers and the three thousand ocean nymphs.

Hyperion was the Titan of light, the father of the sun, the moon, and the dawn.

Mnemosyne was the Titaness of memory and the mother of the Muses. Zeus fathered the Muses.

Themis was the Titaness of justice and order. She gave birth to the Fates and the seasons.

Iapetus was the Titan who fathered Prometheus, Epimetheus, and Atlas.

Other Titans include ***Coeus*** and ***Crius.*** Other Titanesses include ***Phoebe*** and ***Thea.*** Their attributes and functions were either forgotten or insignificant.

Like the original twelve Titans, their children and grandchildren were also called Titans.

Prometheus was the wisest Titan, a benefactor to mankind, whom he created. His name means "forethought." Originally an ally of Zeus, he later tricked Zeus and was chained in the Caucasus Mountains, where an eagle fed upon his liver daily.

Epimetheus was a stupid Titan whose name means "afterthought." He accepted the gift of Pandora from Zeus; and Pandora, the first woman, unleashed all the evils of the world on mankind.

Atlas, for warring against Zeus, was forced to bear the vault of the heavens upon his shoulders at the edge of the world.

OTHER PRIMORDIAL DEITIES

Eros, along with Gaea, was the child of Chaos in early Greek mythology. He represented the creative principle of attraction that brings beings together, establishes friendships and marriages, creates cities, and so on. In later myths he was the son of Aphrodite and represented lust.

The ***Cyclopes*** were one-eyed monsters, the children of Gaea and Uranus. There were at first three of these storm-demons, and they represented the thunder, lightning, and the thunderbolt. They helped Zeus against the Titans.

The ***Hecatoncheires*** were three more monsters produced by Gaea and Uranus. Each had fifty heads and a hundred arms of prodigious strength. These creatures represented the cataclysmic forces of nature. ***Briareus*** was distinguished by the fact that he once served as Zeus's bodyguard. Together they helped Zeus defeat the rebellious Titans.

The ***Giants*** were generated by Uranus' blood when Cronus mutilated him. Eventually they became powerful enough to attack the whole Olympian order and were vanquished only after an earth-shattering battle.

The ***Furies,*** who pursued and punished sinners, also sprang from the blood of Uranus. Specifically, they punished matricides.

THE OLYMPIAN GODS

Zeus was the supreme deity of the Greeks and was depicted as a robust, mature man with a flowing beard. At first a storm-god who wielded the thunderbolt, Zeus became the All-Father who populated the heavens and the earth by his promiscuous liaisons; and he finally became the grand dispenser of justice. His palace was on Mount Olympus, together with the homes of the other Olympians. ***Jupiter*** and ***Jove*** were his Latin names.

Hera was the jealous wife and sister of Zeus, the protectress of marriage and childbirth. In several myths she was quite vindictive toward those with whom Zeus fell in love. Her Latin name was ***Juno.***

Poseidon, a brother of Zeus, was lord of the sea and a god of horses. A wrathful, moody god, he carried a trident and traveled in the company of sea nymphs and monsters of the deep. His Latin name was ***Neptune.***

Demeter was Zeus's full sister, a goddess of vegetation and fertility. She had various lovers, including Zeus, and a daughter, Persephone, who was taken by Hades. In Demeter's grief the earth grew barren, and only when her daughter returned to her for six months of each year did the earth become fruitful. Her Latin name was ***Ceres.***

Apollo, the son of Zeus, was the god of light, of intelligence, of healing, and of the arts. His most important shrine was at Delphi, where an oracle prophesied. Apollo had several love affairs and a few rejections that he punished. He was also called ***Phoebus Apollo.***

Artemis was Apollo's twin sister and a daughter of Zeus. The goddess of chastity, she was a virgin huntress who was shown carrying a bow and a quiver of arrows. By some quirk she also presided over childbirth and was associated with the moon. Her name in Latin was ***Diana.***

Aphrodite, the goddess of love and beauty, was either born of the sea-foam or was the daughter of Zeus. She represented sex, affection, and the power of attraction that binds people together. According to some myths Hephaestus was her husband, Ares her lover, and Eros her son. Aphrodite's Latin counterpart was ***Venus,*** a more erotic goddess.

Athena was the virgin goddess of wisdom, a warrior who sprang fully armed from the head of Zeus after he had swallowed the Titaness Metis. She was also a goddess of the arts and the guardian of Athens. Her chief traits were prudence and valor. She was sometimes called ***Pallas Athena.*** Athena's Latin name was ***Minerva.***

Hestia was the mild virgin goddess of the hearth, the family, and peace. She was Zeus's sister. Her Latin name was ***Vesta.***

Ares, the bullying god of war, was the son of Zeus and Hera. A brutal deity who delighted in slaughter and looting, he was also a coward. In his adulterous affair with Aphrodite, Ares was caught and exposed to ridicule by her husband, Hephaestus. His Latin name was ***Mars.***

Hephaestus was the lame, ugly god of the crafts, a skilled artisan who created many wonderful things. He was injured by his father Zeus for defending Hera in a quarrel. He was identified with the Latin god ***Vulcan,*** a deity of volcanic fire.

Hermes, the cleverest of the Olympian gods, ruled wealth and good fortune, was the patron of commerce and thievery, promoted fertility, and guided men on journeys. He was herald and messenger of the gods, a conductor of souls to the netherworld, and a god of sleep. Hermes was the son of Zeus and was depicted with a helmet, winged sandals, and the caduceus. ***Mercury*** was his Latin name.

Hades was lord of the underworld, the region of the dead. Since he was a brother of Zeus, he was sometimes included among the Olympians. He was a stern, dark, inexorable god, and his kingdom was gray and lifeless. He abducted Persephone, the daughter of Demeter, and made her his queen. His Latin names were ***Dis*** and ***Pluto.***

OTHER GODS

Hebe, the daughter of Zeus and Hera, was the goddess of youth and acted as a cupbearer to the gods.

As a youth, ***Ganymede*** was abducted by Zeus in the form of an eagle that carried the boy to Olympus. There Zeus gave him immortality, made him his lover, and established him as a cupbearer.

Iris was the goddess of the rainbow and sometimes a messenger of the gods.

The ***Three Graces*** presided over banquets and festivities. They represented splendor, mirth, and good cheer.

The ***Nine Muses*** were part of Apollo's retinue and were the daughters of Mnemosyne, or memory. These were goddesses of inspiration: ***Clio*** of history, ***Melpomene*** of tragedy, ***Urania*** of astronomy, ***Thalia*** of comedy, ***Terpsichore*** of dance, ***Calliope*** of epic poetry, ***Erato*** of love verse, ***Euterpe*** of lyric poems, and ***Polyhymnia*** of sacred songs.

Persephone was the lovely daughter of Zeus and Demeter, a goddess of springtime. After Hades abducted her she became the queen of the underworld. ***Proserpina*** was her Latin name.

Dionysus, a fertility god and a god of the vine, was the son of Zeus and Semele. He served to liberate the emotions and to inspire men with joy. Like the grape vine, he suffered death but was resurrected. His female worshipers were the frenzied Maenads. Yet out of his celebration grew the tragic theater. He was also known as ***Bacchus,*** Latin ***Liber,*** a god of drunkenness.

Pan, the son of Hermes, was the god of flocks. He had the torso and head of a man, but the hindquarters and horns of a goat. A marvelous musician, he played the pipes and pursued various nymphs, all of whom rejected him for his ugliness.

The ***Satyrs*** were originally men with horses' haunches and tails, two-legged as opposed to the four-legged Centaurs. But in Roman times they were confused with ***Fauns,*** or goat-men who roamed the woods.

The ***Centaurs*** were principally savage beasts, half-horse and half-man. ***Chiron*** was the exception, a Centaur famous for his virtue and wisdom.

The ***Dryads*** were tree-nymphs and had beautiful female shapes. There were also mountain nymphs, wood nymphs, stream nymphs, and sea nymphs, all in female form.

The ***Gorgons*** were three hideous dragonish sisters that could change men to stone at a glance. ***Medusa*** was the most famous one.

The ***Sirens*** were sisters who sat on rocks by the sea and lured sailors to their doom by singing to them.

Helios was the sun god, but he did not play a large part in Greek mythology.

Aeolus was the custodian of the four winds.

Castor and ***Polydeuces*** (or ***Pollux***) were famous twins who protected sailors. Polydeuces' brotherly devotion when Castor died made their names a by-word for fraternal affection.

Proteus, the son or attendant of Poseidon, had the ability to prophesy and to change his shape at will.

Triton was the trumpeter of the sea and was depicted blowing a large conch shell.

The ***Fates*** were three powerful goddesses who determined the lives of men. ***Clotho*** wove the thread of life; ***Lachesis*** measured it out; and ***Atropos*** cut it off with her scissors of death.

MYTHICAL GREEK GEOGRAPHY

At the center of the earth towered Mount Olympus, where the gods lived and held court. Sometimes Olympus was thought of as the actual mountain in Greece, but more often it was a lofty region in the heavens.

Around the earth ran a limitless river called Ocean. On the northern shores of this river lived the Hyperboreans, a fortunate race of men who never knew care, toil, illness, or old age. This community was isolated from the rest of the world, being unapproachable by land or sea. It enjoyed perpetual light and warmth.

To the West lay Hesperia, the land of the evening star, where the golden apples of Hera were guarded by the dragon Ladon and by seven immortal maidens, the Hesperides. The western lands and seas were populated with monstrous beings: the one-eyed Cyclopes, the cannibalistic Laestrygonians, Scylla and Charybdis, the Sirens, and the Titan Atlas. But also to the far west lay the Elysian Fields, or Isles of the Blessed, where certain favored mortals went when they died.

In the far south were the Ethiopians, a lucky, virtuous people with whom the gods banqueted. And in the East were the barbarians, or non-Greek-speaking races to whom the blessings of civilization were unknown.

Beneath the disk of the earth was Tartarus, where the Titans were confined, a vast, nebulous realm of darkness. Between earth and Tartarus was the underworld kingdom of Hades, the ruler of the dead. The entrance to this realm was guarded by Cerberus, the three-headed dog. And once the departed spirits passed they had to be ferried across the River Styx by Charon, the foul-tempered boatman. The place was thought of as cavernous and dim, a joyless abode in which the dead gradually faded into nothingness.

THE BEGINNINGS

CREATION

In the beginning there was only Chaos, an empty void. But somehow this enormous vacancy gave birth to Gaea, the earth, to Tartarus, the great region beneath the earth, and to Eros, the shining god of love and attraction. Chaos also bore Erebus, the darkness of the netherworld, and Night, the darkness over the earth. Then Erebus slept with Night, who gave birth to Ether, the heavenly light, and to Day, the earthly light. Later Night alone produced such beings as Doom, Fate, Death, Sleep, Dreams, Nemesis, and a long list of other atrocities that steal upon men in darkness.

Meanwhile Gaea, without help, gave birth to Uranus, the starry sky, to the Mountains, and to Pontus, the sterile sea. Uranus then became Gaea's mate and equal, for he covered her on all sides. This primordial couple, sky and earth, produced the twelve Titans, the three towering wheel-eyed Cyclopes, and the three terrible Hecatoncheires with fifty heads and a hundred arms apiece.

However, Uranus proved to be a harsh husband and father. Each of the Hecatoncheires hated him, and he hated them in return. In his anger Uranus pushed them back into Gaea's womb and kept them there. Gaea writhed in pain at this and plotted revenge upon her mate. She fashioned a flint sickle and called upon her other children to avenge her. The Titans and Cyclopes recoiled in fear of their father, and only the last-born Titan, Cronus, was daring enough.

That night when Uranus came to lie with Gaea the crafty Cronus was hiding in ambush. He grabbed his father's genitals and severed them with his mother's sickle. As the blood fell to earth the Furies, who punish crimes, the Ash-Tree Nymphs, and the race of Giants were created. Cronus heaved the members into the sea, and from the foam arose Aphrodite, the beautiful goddess of love, who floated along and stepped ashore at Cyprus. The mutilated Uranus either withdrew forever from the earth or else he perished. But before he did so he promised that Cronus and the other Titans would be punished.

After confining the Cyclopes and the Hecatoncheires to Tartarus, Cronus established his reign. He married his sister Rhea, and under his lordship the Titans produced many offspring. Yet Cronus could not allow his own children to survive, for both Gaea and Uranus had prophesied that Cronus would be supplanted by a son. When Rhea, his wife, gave birth to the gods and goddesses Cronus swallowed Hestia, Demeter, Hera, Hades, and Poseidon shortly after each was born. Rhea was furious and took pains to save her sixth child, Zeus, from his father. She bore Zeus in secret and then gave Cronus a stone wrapped in swaddling bands to swallow instead.

Attended by nymphs, Zeus grew to manhood on Crete. Cronus, meanwhile, was growing old. So Zeus sought advice on how to defeat him from the Titaness Metis, who prepared an emetic potion. Disguised as a cupbearer, Zeus gave this potion to Cronus, who vomited up Zeus's brothers and sisters, as well as the stone Rhea had given him. The gods were alive and unhurt, and together with Zeus they triumphed over Cronus and bound him in Tartarus. Zeus then set up the stone at Parnassus, a monument to his victory over the Titan king.

Zeus's triumph, however, was far from secure. The other Titans, with the exception of Prometheus and Oceanus, rebelled under these upstart gods. For ten years the fighting lasted, a cosmos-shaking battle in which the elements of nature raged without check. Neither the gods nor the Titans could secure a decisive victory. But then Zeus went down to Tartarus and released the Cyclopes and the hundred-handed monsters. The Cyclopes awarded Zeus their weapons of thunder and lightning, and the Hecatoncheires pelted the Titans with boulders. And at last the Titans were defeated. Zeus imprisoned them in Tartarus, and he condemned the rebel Atlas to stand forever at the edge of the world and bear the heavens on his shoulders.

Gaea was enraged at the downfall of her children, the Titans. And through her union with Tartarus she gave birth to one last monster, Typhoeus, a dragon with a hundred heads that never rested. Terrified, most of the gods fled. But Zeus was captured and confined. Released by Hermes, Zeus finally destroyed the dragon by hurling lightning at it again and again, and by burying it under Etna in Sicily.

There was one more attempt to dislodge Zeus and the other Olympians from their mastery of the world. The Giants, who had sprouted from Uranus' blood, were dissatisfied, so they laid siege to Olympus by piling mountain upon mountain in an attempt to scale it. It required all the prowess of the gods and the assistance of the mortal Heracles to subdue and kill the Giants. Having vanquished the Titans, the dragon Typhoeus, and the Giants, the rule of the Olympians was undisputed.

That version of the creation was taken largely from Hesiod, a Greek poet of the seventh century B.C.. But here is an earlier story by way of contrast.

Eurynome, the goddess of all creation, arose from Chaos and separated the sea from the sky. Then, dancing naked upon the waves, she created the wind and rubbed it in her hands to create the serpent Ophion, who made love to her. Pregnant, Eurynome became a dove and laid the World Egg, and Ophion coiled about the Egg and hatched it. This Egg brought forth the cosmos and everything in it. Then Eurynome and Ophion settled on Olympus, but their union was unhappy. When Ophion proclaimed himself the Creator, Eurynome banished him to the netherworld. Finally Eurynome established the seven planets, each with a Titan and Titaness to rule it. When man appeared he sprang from the soil, and the first man, Pelasgus, taught the others to eat acorns, build huts, and make a rude garment.

Commentary

The first version of the creation is intensely masculine and crude. The primary forces generate their opposites. Thus vacancy creates solidity, darkness creates light, the earth creates the sky and the sea, the first crime creates a goddess of love. Further, these forces are conceived as having sexes, and they copulate the way human beings do, and the female elements give birth to newer forces, and those forces have vague personalities.

Apart from childbearing, Gaea and her daughter Rhea have one important function. In anger they help their sons dethrone their own husbands. The relationship between the sexes is troubled, and the decisive factor in losing control of the world is mistreating one's children. The forces of nature are rendered in terms of the human family, which makes the creation both understandable and dramatic.

The most notable feature of this myth, however, is the drive for power and dominance. Uranus confines the mightiest of his offspring to Gaea's belly. Cronus castrates his father and the new generation of Titans takes over. Then Cronus consolidates his power by imprisoning his non-Titan brothers and by swallowing his own children. Zeus, his son, in turn dethrones him, and then must fight the Titans, the dragon, and the Giants to secure his own rule. In one myth even Zeus is warned that a hypothetical son by Thetis may defeat him. Power is the primary drive here.

But this view of the world is not really pessimistic, for each generation of deities is an improvement over the last one. The Olympian gods under Zeus are the most enlightened generation, and only the ablest survive.

It is thought that the Titans were the old gods of Greece, and that the gods of the Indo-European invaders superseded them, particularly Zeus. Yet what is important about this story is that conflict is shown to be a cosmic principle. By fighting alone does the world progress, since only in that way can the victors, gods or men, establish their supremacy. And that supremacy is always subject to question in the end. Force determines who keeps power. Nevertheless, this view of the world in terms of conflict gave Greek civilization an extremely dramatic character.

It is precisely drama that is lacking in the early, Pelasgian account of the creation. There a female deity is all-important, perhaps reflecting a matriarchal society. Eurynome is playful in creating her wind-mate Ophion, and she is vicious in disposing of him when he claims to be the Creator. She can live without a masculine god, being self-sufficient. In this myth things seem to happen accidentally, from Eurynome's birth to the creation of man. There is no unifying principle at work here beyond that of feminine playfulness and pique. Given the two stories of the creation, it is easy to see why the one told by Hesiod achieved dominance, for it stemmed from a race of fighters.

PROMETHEUS AND MAN

The clever Titan Prometheus and his stupid brother Epimetheus were spared imprisonment in Tartarus because they had kept their neutrality in the war between the Olympians and the Titans. According to one tradition Prometheus shaped man out of mud, and Athena breathed life into the clay figure. Once man was created, however, Prometheus allowed his scatterbrained brother, Epimetheus, to dispense various qualities to the animals and man. So Epimetheus began by giving the best traits to the animals—swiftness, courage, cunning, stealth, and the like—and he wound up with nothing to give to man. So Prometheus took the matter in hand and gave man an upright posture like the gods. And this gift enabled him to survive.

Prometheus had little love for the Olympians, who had banished his fellow Titans to the depths of Tartarus. His primary affection was for man. Now man had to make animal sacrifices to the gods, but a certain portion of the animal was to be given to the gods and a certain portion to man. Zeus had to decide. So Prometheus made two piles. He wrapped the bones in juicy fat and he hid the meat under the ugly hide. Zeus chose the bones wrapped in fat, much to his anger.

In retaliation Zeus deprived man of fire. But Prometheus was not to be stopped. He went up to heaven and lighted his torch at the sun and carried it back to earth. Zeus was livid with rage when he saw that man had fire. He ordered that Hephaestus create a mortal of stunning beauty, and when Hephaestus had done so the gods gave this new creature many gifts. But Hermes gave it a deceptive heart and a lying tongue. This was the first woman, Pandora, and a worse calamity never befell man.

Prometheus had warned his brother Epimetheus about accepting gifts from Zeus. Yet when Epimetheus saw this radiant creature Pandora he could not resist her. She had brought with her a jar that she was forbidden to open. But being a woman, her curiosity won out. As she opened the lid a multitude of evils flew out and scattered over the world to afflict man. Still, there remained in the jar one consolation for man—Hope. With all the misery Pandora had unleashed hope was the only thing that could keep mankind going.

For Prometheus, Zeus reserved a special punishment. In addition to anger at the sacrifice trick and the theft of fire, Zeus knew that Prometheus held the secret of the god who would finally dethrone him. In defiance Prometheus would not tell the secret. Zeus had Prometheus chained to a rock in the Caucasus, and every day he sent an eagle to peck out the Titan's liver, which grew back again every night. This agony was drawn out for ages. There were two conditions on which he could be released from the rock: first, that an immortal must suffer death for Prometheus, and, second, that a mortal must slay the eagle and unchain him. And in time the Centaur Chiron did agree to die for him, while Heracles killed the eagle and unbound him.

THE FIVE AGES OF MAN AND THE FLOOD

According to another story the gods created man, and man existed on earth while the Titan Cronus ruled. The first race of men lived in complete happiness. During that Golden Age men were free from pain, toil, and old age. Dying was as easy as falling asleep. They enjoyed the fruits of the earth in plenty. And once this race had died out these mortals remained as spirits to protect men from evil.

Then the gods created the men of the Silver Age, who were far inferior. These men remained children for a hundred years under the dominance of their mothers. And when they finally matured they died off shortly because of their foolishness. In this age men had to work, and the year was divided into seasons so that men knew cold and heat. Crime and impiety also had their beginnings in this period, so Zeus put an end to this race.

Next Zeus created the men of the Bronze Age out of ash spears. These men were mighty, tall, and ferocious, a violent race of warriors who worked in metal and produced a few rudiments of civilization. In the end these men destroyed themselves with their warfare.

The next period was the Heroic Age, a time of notable heroes and deeds. Heracles and Jason, Theseus, and the great men of the Trojan War existed then. As a tribute to them Zeus established the Elysian Fields as a resting place for their spirits after death.

Still not discouraged, Zeus created the men of the Iron Age, the worst race ever to appear on earth and one destined to become totally depraved. Hard work, trouble, pain, and weariness were the lot of this group of men, which still exists. At the last the gods will totally abandon this vicious race, leaving it in utter pain.

At one time Zeus was so thoroughly disgusted with man and his impious, evil ways that he decided to annihilate the species with a deluge. Prometheus, who was still at large then, warned his son Deucalion to prepare a chest. When the rains began to fall Deucalion and his wife Pyrrha climbed into the chest, which was loaded with provisions, and they floated on the ocean that drowned the rest of the world. After ten days the flood subsided, and the chest came to rest on Mount Parnassus. When they emerged, Deucalion and Pyrrha offered a sacrifice to Zeus and asked him to restore the human race. The couple also went to Delphi and prayed to the Titaness of Justice, who told them to cast the bones of their mother behind them. At first this command mystified them, but Deucalion had an inspiration. His mother's bones must be the stones that lay upon the earth, for the earth had given birth to mankind. As Deucalion started casting stones behind him they became men, and as Pyrrha cast stones behind her they became women. In this manner the human race was reborn.

Commentary

Many parts of these legends derive from Hesiod, who wrote of the beginnings of the world. One feature is common to each legend—the idea of mankind's frailty in the face of destruction. Sometimes man brings calamity upon himself by impiety or murderousness, but other times it may be the result of events over which he has no control. Zeus is a vindictive god here who punishes man not merely for man's own misdeeds but also for those of Prometheus.

Prometheus, of course, is a heroic figure as a friend of mankind. He is the stubborn rebel against Zeus's terrible power, and his personal sacrifice on behalf of humanity is much to his credit. Even his trickery in the matter of the sacrifice is seen as admirable. The ancient Greeks admired cunning and trickery. Many of their gods and heroes possess a gift for deception.

While being a libel on women, the story of Pandora reveals a double feeling about females. On the one hand, they are irresistible, and on the other, they are the cause of men's woes. Such a story could only arise in a culture where men were dominant. The traits that are stressed as inherent in women—a treacherous heart and a lying tongue—are the natural weapons of a subjugated sex.

The tale of the five ages of man shows a deep pessimism about man's development. While each generation of gods is an improvement on the last, each new race of man is inferior to the last one. Man degenerates from eon to eon. No story could be more at odds with our almost universal belief in man's evolution from savagery to civilization. Yet be that as it may, the myth reflects the idea of the paradisiacal condition of early man, an idea which is also behind the biblical legend of Eden.

The story of the Flood, too, has its biblical counterpart in the tale of Noah. This myth is very widespread. Versions of it exist throughout the globe. The notion of a flood wiping out almost all of mankind conflicts with the prevalent idea that geological changes take place gradually. Nevertheless, the myth of the Flood reveals a belief in the cataclysmic powers of nature, powers that can destroy man if the gods so choose.

LOVES OF ZEUS

After deposing Cronus, Zeus and his brothers drew lots to see which portion of the world would be ruled by each. Zeus thus gained the mastery of the sky, Poseidon of the seas, and Hades of the underworld. It was also decreed that earth, and Olympus in particular, would be common to all three. In addition to having the most power, Zeus gained another advantage from his position as a sky god, since it allowed him free access to any beauty that took his fancy. Indeed, as a sky god it was expected of him to fecundate the earth; and neither goddess, nymph, nor mortal was able to resist his advances, for the most part.

Zeus had had other wives before Hera. The first was Metis (Wisdom), whom Zeus swallowed just before she gave birth to Athena because he knew that her second child would dethrone him. Yet in order to allow Athena to live, as Metis' firstborn, Zeus had Hephaestus take an axe and cleave his forehead open, and from Zeus's head sprang Athena, fully armed. By swallowing Metis, however, Zeus had gained wisdom as part of his intrinsic nature.

His second wife, Themis (Divine Justice), gave birth to the Seasons, to Wise Laws, to Human Justice, to Peace, and to the Fates. His third wife was Eurynome, an ocean nymph, and she bore the three Graces. Zeus then was attracted by his sister Demeter, who resisted him. But he violated her in the form of a bull, and from their union came Persephone. His next wife was the Titaness Mnemosyne (Memory), who produced the Nine Muses. Leto was said to be one of Zeus's consorts. She gave birth to Artemis and Apollo after a good deal of persecution at Hera's hands.

Zeus finally became enamored of the goddess who was to become his permanent wife—Hera. After courting her unsuccessfully he changed himself into a disheveled cuckoo. When Hera took pity on the bird and held it to her breast, Zeus resumed his true form and ravished her. Hera then decided to marry him to cover her shame, and the two had a resplendent wedding worthy of the gods. It took no great foresight to see that their marriage was bound to be quarrelsome and unhappy, given Zeus's lust and Hera's jealousy.

Their union brought forth four children: Hebe, the cupbearer to the gods; Ares, the god of war; Ilithyia, a goddess of childbearing; and Hephaestus, the craftsman of the gods. Perhaps in retaliation for Zeus's giving birth to Athena. Hera claimed that Hephaestus was virgin-born. Zeus never cared much for his two legitimate sons, Ares and Hephaestus. And his two legitimate daughters were almost nonentities. One time Hephaestus interfered in a quarrel between Zeus and Hera, siding with his mother. In a rage Zeus hurled his ugly son down from Olympus to the isle of Lemnos, crippling him forever.

The arguments between Zeus and Hera were fairly frequent. As Zeus continued to have one affair after another, Hera could not punish him because he was much stronger than she was. But she could avenge herself on the females with whom Zeus dallied, and she often took full advantage of this.

A number of Zeus's affairs resulted in new gods and godesses. His liaison with Metis, of course, produced the warrior goddess of wisdom and courage, Athena. One night as Hera slumbered, Zeus made love to one of the Pleiades, Maia, who gave birth to the tricky messenger of the gods, Hermes. By some accounts Zeus begat the goddess of love, Aphrodite, on the Titaness Dione. And when he took Leto as his consort he must have been married to Hera, for Hera persecuted Leto by condemning her to bear her children in a land of complete darkness. After traveling throughout Greece, Leto finally gave birth painlessly to Artemis, the virgin huntress, on the isle of Ortygia. Nine days later she gave birth to Apollo, the god of light and inspiration, on the island of Delos. Each of these new gods and goddesses were fullfledged Olympians, having had two divine parents.

One important god, however, had Zeus as a father and a mortal woman as a mother. This was Dionysus, the vine god of ecstasy, who was never granted Olympian status. His mother was the Theban princess, Semele. Zeus visited her one night in the darkness, and she knew a divine being was present and she slept with him. When it turned out that Semele was pregnant she boasted that Zeus was the father. Hera learned of this and came to Semele disguised as her nurse. Hera asked how she knew the father was Zeus, and Semele had no proof. So Hera suggested that Semele ask to see this god in his full glory. The next time Zeus visited the girl he was so delighted with her that he promised her anything she wanted. She wanted to see Zeus fully revealed. Since Zeus never broke his word, he sadly showed himself forth in his true essence, a burst of glory that utterly destroyed Semele, burning her up. Yet Zeus spared her unborn infant, sewing it up inside his thigh until it was able to emerge as the god Dionysus. His birth from Zeus's thigh alone conferred immortality on him.

Among Zeus's offspring were great heroes such as Perseus, Castor and Polydeuces, the great Heracles. Some were founders of cities or countries, like Epaphus, who founded Memphis; Arcas, who became king of Arcadia; Lacedaemon, the king of Lacedaemon and founder of Sparta. One was the wisest lawgiver of his age, the first Minos. Another was a fabulous beauty, the famous Helen of Troy. And one was a monster of depravity: Tantalus, who served up his son Pelops as food to the gods. As a general rule Zeus's mortal children were distinguished for one reason or another.

On occasion their mothers were notable for something besides merely attracting Zeus with their beauty. Leda, for example, after being visited by Zeus in the form of a swan, gave birth to an egg from which came Helen and Clytemnestra, and

Castor and Polydeuces. But since Leda's husband Tyndarus also made love to her shortly after Zeus, the exact paternity of these quadruplets was subject to question.

Poor Io was famous for her long persecution at the hands of Hera. Zeus fell in love with Io and seduced her under a thick blanket of cloud to keep Hera from learning of it. But Hera was no fool; she flew down from Olympus, dispersed the cloud, and found Zeus standing by a white heifer, who of course was Io. Hera calmly asked Zeus if she could have this animal, and Zeus gave it to her, reluctant to go into an explanation. But Hera knew it was Io, so she put her under guard. The watchman Argus with a hundred eyes was put in charge. Eventually Zeus sent his son Hermes to deliver Io from Argus, which was very difficult because Argus never slept. In disguise Hermes managed to put Argus to sleep with stories and flute-playing, and then Hermes killed him. As a memorial to Argus, Hera set his eyes in the tail of her pet bird, the peacock. But Hera was furious and sent a gadfly to chase Io over the earth. Still in the form of a heifer, Io ran madly from country to country, tormented by the stinging insect. At one point she came across Prometheus chained to his rock in the Caucasus, and the two victims of divine injustice discussed her plight. Prometheus pointed out that her sufferings were far from over, but that after long journeying she would reach the Nile, be changed back into human shape, give birth to Epaphus, the son of Zeus, and receive many honors. And from her descendants would come Heracles, the man who would set Prometheus free.

If Hera was diligent about punishing Io, Europa escaped her wrath scot-free. One morning this lovely daughter of the king of Sidon had a dream in which two continents in female form laid claim to her. Europa belonged to Asia by birth, but the other continent, which was nameless, said that Zeus would give Europa to her. Later, while Europa and her girl companions were frolicking by the sea, Zeus was smitten with the princess and changed himself into a marvelous bull of great handsomeness. He approached the girls so gently that they ran to play with him. Zeus knelt down and Europa climbed on his back. Then the bull charged into the sea, and on the sea journey Europa and Zeus were accompanied by strange sea creatures: Nereids, Tritons, and Poseidon himself. Europa then realized that the bull was a god in disguise and she begged Zeus not to desert her. Zeus replied that he was taking her to Crete, his original home, and that her sons from this union would be grand kings who would rule all men. In time Europa gave birth to Minos and Rhadamanthus, wise rulers who became judges in the netherworld after death. And Europa gave her name to a continent.

Despite his conquests Zeus was not always successful in his amorous pursuits. The nymph Asteria managed to resist him only by the most desperate means—changing herself into a quail, flinging herself into the sea, and becoming the floating island of Ortygia. On one occasion Zeus himself renounced the nymph Thetis when he learned that she would give birth to a son greater than its father. Further, Zeus's infatuations were not limited to women, for when he fell in love with the youthful Ganymede he had the boy abducted by his eagle and brought up to Olympus to serve as cupbearer.

Commentary

In previous sections we have seen Zeus's power as king of the gods and a dispenser of justice to men, but here we see him as a procreator. As H. J. Rose has pointed out, the Greeks had a choice of making Zeus either polygamous or promiscuous, because the role of All-Father was indispensable to him. Zeus had acquired wives as his worship spread from locality to locality and he had to marry each provincial earth goddess. However, polygamy was foreign to the Greeks and unacceptable, so they had to make him promiscuous. The same majestic god who fathered seven of the great Olympians also fathered a number of human beings, and many ruling or powerful families traced their lineage to Zeus. So if his battles with Hera and his deceptions lessened his dignity, that was the price the Greeks paid for their illustrious family trees.

The myths about Zeus are primarily concerned with establishing his mastery over gods and men. His predominance in the Olympian pantheon is largely asserted by the fact that he fathered seven of the major gods. Once again we see the humanization of the gods. Zeus and Hera have distinct personalities and a realistic family situation. Everything they do has an understandable motive. Thus, when Zeus changes himself into bestial forms he does so to satisfy his lust. The Greeks had a driving passion for order. They continually rationalized their myths, tried to explain obscurities, and attempted to make the fantastic elements more believable. However, in making their gods humanly comprehensible they tended to trivialize them as well, depriving them of some of their original power and mystery. One could fill several gossip columns with spicy anecdotes about the Greek gods, as though they were immortal versions of the International Set. The following myths about the gods show human qualities projected onto divinities, and many of those qualities are not of a very high moral level. Pride, greed, lust, trickery are prominent features of the Greek gods.

POSEIDON

Zeus's brother Poseidon gained control of the sea as his portion of the world. And like the sea he had a stormy, violent nature. Poseidon built a palace in the watery depths and sought a wife who could live there. At one time he courted Thetis, the sea nymph, but he gave her up when he learned that she would bear a son greater than its father. Then he courted Amphitrite, another sea nymph, but she disliked him and fled far away. Poseidon sent messengers to fetch her, and one of them, a dolphin, was able to persuade her to marry the lord of the sea. Yet the marriage was not very happy for her because Poseidon, like Zeus, persisted in extramarital affairs. In one case Amphitrite transformed her husband's mistress into a loathsome, barking monster.

Not satisfied with lordship over the sea, Poseidon coveted earthly realms as well. In his dispute with Athena for dominion over Athens, the two gods had a contest as to which one could give the Athenians the best gift. Poseidon shoved his trident into the Acropolis and produced a flowing stream or a horse. Undismayed, Athena gave the Athenians an olive tree. And Poseidon challenged Athena to combat. Zeus, however, demanded that the quarrel be submitted to the arbitration of the gods. Then the male gods sided with Poseidon, while the goddesses favored Athena. Since Zeus withheld his vote, the goddesses were in the majority so that Athena won. But Poseidon flooded the country around Athens in retaliation. His other bids for power were unsuccessful, too, as he tried to seize Naxos from Dionysus, Aegina from Zeus, Corinth from Helios, and Argolis from Hera. His quarrelsome greed made him rather unpopular with the other Olympians.

ATHENA

As a warrior goddess, Athena was depicted in long, flowing robes, wearing a helmet and holding a spear in one hand and a winged victory in the other. She was a redoubtable fighter and took an active part in the war against the Giants and in the Trojan War. Unlike Ares, who was rashly bellicose and sometimes cowardly in battle, Athena had a cool, prudent courage that aided her in various undertakings. A protectress of heroes, she assisted Perseus, Heracles, Bellerophon, Achilles, and Odysseus in their various exploits. Nonetheless, Athena never felt the pangs of love and she remained a virgin. Once Hephaestus tried to violate her, but Athena managed to defend herself and Hephaestus spilled his seed on the ground, which gave birth to Erichthonius. Athena took care of this infant, and eventually he became king of Athens and made Athena the chief deity of the city. Another time Teiresias accidentally found Athena bathing, so she blinded him. But at his mother's pleading she gave him the gift of prophecy to compensate for blindness.

Athena was of great benefit to mankind as a goddess of the peaceful crafts. Among her inventions were the trumpet, the flute, the pot, the rake, the plow, the yoke, the bridle, the ship, and the chariot. She also invented mathematics and excelled in the arts of cooking, spinning, and weaving. She particularly prided herself on the ability to weave, and when a princess from Colophon, Arachne, produced a flawless tapestry the angry goddess changed her into a spider. Although Athena invented the flute, she became disgusted with it when Hera and Aphrodite laughed at her swollen cheeks as she played it, so she threw the flute away and pronounced a curse on it. The satyr, Marsyas, picked the flute up and acquired great skill on the instrument. Apollo became jealous of Marsyas' ability and challenged him to a music contest. When Apollo won he flayed the poor satyr to death and nailed his skin to a tree.

Definitely not a goddess to be trifled with, Athena was once assaulted by the furious Ares, who struck her on her invincible breastplate, the aegis. Athena then picked up a huge boulder and flung it at the god of war, causing him to crumple to the ground. Yet despite her rather mannish character, she was merciful in legal disputes and preferred peaceful ways of settling quarrels.

APOLLO

The god Apollo had many functions. As a deity of light he helped to ripen crops, destroy pests, and heal illnesses. Yet he could also be deadly as he shot his terrible arrows and created plagues. A god of prohecy, he had many oracular shrines, the chief one being at Delphi. He was a shepherd god as well and protected flocks. The master of the lyre and song, Apollo was especially vain about his musical prowess, and kept the Muses as part of his retinue. Beyond this he was a builder and a god of colonies. In his representations he was depicted as a nude, beardless young man of handsome proportions, and he was often shown with a bow and quiver or a lyre.

Hera had sent the serpent Python to pursue Apollo's mother, Leto, during her pregnancy. Four days after he was born Apollo called for a bow and arrows. When Hephaestus had furnished these Apollo went in search of Python. At length he managed to trap the serpent in a gorge by Parnassus and promptly slew the monster with his arrows. Apollo then had to purify himself, going into temporary exile in Thessaly.

On two occasions Apollo aroused the anger of his father, Zeus. The first time he had acted in consort with Hera, Poseidon, and other gods to dethrone Zeus, who had been unusually high-handed. Zeus was captured and bound to his couch, where the rebels threatened to kill him. However, the nymph Thetis brought Briareus, the fifty-headed monster, to guard Zeus, and this effectively quashed the rebellion. In vengeance Zeus hung Hera by her heels from Olympus, and he sent Apollo and Poseidon to a year's servitude under King Laomedon. And when Laomedon refused to pay them their rightful wages for building Troy and tending the royal oxen, Apollo visited Laomedon's kingdom with the plague and Poseidon sent a sea-monster to ravage the land.

The other time Apollo angered Zeus occurred when Zeus killed Apollo's son, Asclepius, for resurrecting a dead man. In retaliation Apollo killed Zeus's armorers, the Cyclopes. Zeus would have sent Apollo to Tartarus except that Leto pleaded for her son. Apollo was then given a year's servitude under King Admetus, for whom he performed great services.

After defeating Marsyas in a music contest Apollo had another contest with Pan, the goat-god. Apollo again gained the victory, emerging as the undisputed master musician.

Such a comely, youthful god was usually quite successful with nymphs and women. A randy bachelor, he seduced Phthia, Thalia, Coronis, Aria, Cyrene, and the nymph Dryope, having children by each. But some of his pursuits were failures. Marpessa eluded him. The nymph Daphne was changed into a laurel tree by Mother Earth before Apollo could ravish her. To console himself Apollo made a laurel wreath from her. When the Trojan princess Cassandra rejected him after he gave her the gift of divination, he turned the gift into a curse by making it so that no one would believe her prophecies.

Apollo also fell in love with a handsome boy, Hyacinthus. Zephyrus, the West Wind, fell in love with the boy, too, and became very jealous of Apollo. One day as Apollo was instructing the boy in discus-throwing Zephyrus seized the missile in midair and hurled it against Hyacinthus' head. The boy was killed, but where his blood fell there sprang up the hyacinth flower bearing the boy's initials.

ARTEMIS

The twin sister of Apollo, Artemis was the virgin-huntress, a goddess of the chase and forest creatures. The young also fell under her care, and because her mother Leto had delivered her without pain Artemis was called upon to help in childbirth. She was usually depicted in long robes carrying a bow and quiver, and she was accompanied by a troop of woodland nymphs.

One of those nymphs was Callisto, whom Zeus made love to in the guise of Artemis herself. One account says that when Artemis discovered the poor nymph was pregnant she reached for her bow and an arrow. Just as Artemis was about to kill the hapless girl, Zeus changed Callisto into a bear and set her up in heaven as the constellation of Ursa Major.

Artemis was very secretive about where she bathed, so when the hunter Actaeon came across her and her nymphs in the nude she changed him into a stag and set his own hounds to tear him to pieces.

APHRODITE

Aphrodite was the goddess of love in all its forms, a protectress of marriage, the inspirer of ideal affection, and a deity of abandoned sexuality. Often she was depicted as a voluptuous nude of striking beauty. But as though her natural charms were not enough, she also possessed a magical girdle that rendered her irresistible to gods and mortals alike.

Zeus gave Aphrodite to Hephaestus, the ugly, lame craftsman of the gods, to be his wife. Hephaestus was infatuated with his beautiful bride, but apparently she was less than enchanted with him, for she took the virile Ares, god of war, as her lover. Helios reported her misconduct to Hephaestus, who fashioned a very fine but powerful net and suspended it above his wife's bed. Hephaestus then told his wife he was going away for a few days, and Aphrodite summoned Ares. While the adulterous couple was sporting in bed the net fell, binding the two fast. Hephaestus then called upon the other gods to witness his naked wife and her lover in the trap he had laid. Moreover, he demanded that Zeus return the dowry he had paid for his wife, but Zeus was disgusted with the whole affair and left. Apollo and Hermes jested about how they would not mind being caught in the net with such an attractive goddess; and Poseidon became enamored of Aphrodite and offered to guarantee payment of the dowry, should Ares default. Hephaestus released Ares and never received the dowry, but neither did he divorce his wife. In the end he had to tolerate her infidelities.

From that time on Aphrodite slept with many. She bore children to the gods Hermes, Poseidon, and Dionysus, two of which were sexually abnormal. If Zeus never lay with her he was tempted, and he punished her by making her fall in love with a mortal, the handsome Trojan prince, Anchises. In disguise Aphrodite offered herself to the young man, who made love to her on his bed of furs. In the morning she revealed her true identity, which terrified Anchises. She said that no harm would befall him unless he revealed her secret tryst with him. Naturally Anchises could not help telling about it among his drinking companions, and Zeus hurled a thunderbolt at him that would have killed him had not Aphrodite deflected its course a little. But Anchises could never walk upright again. Yet the result of his union with Aphrodite was Aeneas, a great hero.

Proud of her beauty, Aphrodite took offense when a queen of Cyprus bragged that her daughter was more lovely. Aphrodite infected the girl with an incestuous love for the king, her father. The girl contrived a union with the king and became pregnant. Upon learning that he was the procreator of his daughter's child the king chased the girl in a rage, his sword upraised. And just as he was about to cleave her Aphrodite changed the girl into a tree, and as the sword fell, splitting the tree, a child was born.

Aphrodite took the infant Adonis and entrusted him to Persephone, Queen of the Underworld. He grew into a handsome youth, and Persephone took him for a lover. Aphrodite, on learning of his comeliness, went to the underworld to retrieve Adonis, and a squabble arose between the two goddesses. It was decided through arbitration that each one should have him for a third of the year, and that he should have a third to himself. Dissatisfied with this agreement, Aphrodite seduced Adonis with her magic girdle into remaining with her for the whole year. The angry Persephone reported this situation to Aphrodite's old lover, Ares, who changed himself into a boar and attacked Adonis, killing the youth. As Adonis' blood fell to the ground anemone flowers sprang forth. And since his soul descended to the underworld, Persephone at last had him all to herself. However, Aphrodite petitioned Zeus to allow Adonis to spend the summer months in her company, and Zeus agreed.

HERMES

The cleverest and most precocious god was Hermes. His functions were related to travel for the most part, as a god of the roads, of commerce, of thievery, and an usher of the dead in the netherworld. He was also a phallic god, and pillars with a head called *herms* were set up in front of Greek homes. A god of intelligence, he invented the lyre, the pipes, the musical scale, astronomy, weights and measures, boxing, gymnastics, and the care of olive trees.

Immediately after he was born he went out and killed a tortoise. From its shell Hermes created the lyre, and with it he lulled his mother Maia to sleep, which left him free to do as he pleased. Before long he came across a splendid herd of cattle that belonged to Apollo, so he promptly stole the herd and disguised the tracks so that no one could trace him. When Apollo discovered his loss he went out searching in all directions for the stolen cattle. He even posted a reward. Finally he got wind of their whereabouts and found two cow hides at Hermes' dwelling. Still an infant, Hermes was pretending to sleep. But Apollo insisted on taking him before Zeus.

Zeus was astonished when Apollo accused the babe of thieving his cattle. But Apollo browbeat Hermes into a full confession. After admitting that he had sacrificed the two dead cows to the gods, Hermes promised to deliver the rest of the herd to Apollo. On the way to get the cows Hermes took Apollo home and showed him the lyre he had made. Apollo was so entranced with it that he exchanged the cattle for the lyre. Hermes also demonstrated the pipes he had created, and Apollo told him where he could learn the art of divination in exchange for the pipes. The two gods were fast friends ever after.

Hermes presented himself to Zeus as a new god and promised never to steal or tell a lie again. Zeus then defined his duties as a god of travel and gave Hermes his winged sandals and his staff, the caduceus. In his role as the messenger of the gods he appeared in more myths than any other god, with the possible exception of Zeus.

DEMETER

The grain goddess, Demeter, was a full sister to Zeus and an Olympian deity in her own right. However, as an agricultural goddess her destiny was more closely bound to the earth than to the celestial regions of Olympus. Demeter instituted the Eleusinian Mysteries, a religious cult that apparently believed in reincarnation. Just as the grain springs up every year after its harvest and wintery death, so the members of this cult believed that the human soul would be reborn after the body's death.

Demeter had one daughter, Persephone or Core, whom she adored. Zeus had fathered the girl, and she was strikingly beautiful. The god of the underworld, Hades, desired her. And one day as she was picking flowers Persephone wandered away from her companions to pick a strange but lovely narcissus plant. As she stooped down the earth yawned at her feet and Hades rode out from the bowels of the earth and abducted her. Demeter was heartsick at the loss and searched everywhere for her daughter in vain. After nine days of hunting she found Helios, the sun god, who told her what had happened. Hades had taken the maiden to be his queen, while Zeus had consented to it.

Demeter in her anger abandoned Olympus and came to live on the earth disguised as a crone. She arrived at Eleusis and was taken into the home of Prince Celeus and his wife Metaneira, where she was allowed to nurse their son Demophoön. In return for their hospitality Demeter decided to make the infant immortal by secret rites. Metaneira, however, grew suspicious and burst in upon Demeter as she was burning away the baby's mortal parts. The mother screamed and her son died. Demeter then revealed herself as the goddess, scolding Metaneira and ordering that a temple be built in her honor at Eleusis. The temple was constructed to be Demeter's dwelling place.

Still brooding about her daughter's loss, the goddess laid a curse on the earth that caused every plant to wither. Since nothing would grow, the lands became desolate and inhospitable to life. Zeus started to worry and finally sent Hermes down to the netherworld to fetch Persephone back to her mother. It was decreed, however, that if she partook of any food in the kingdom of the dead she would have to return. Persephone had languished in Hades' realm, eating nothing and grieving. But as Hermes arrived she took a bite of a pomegranate that Hades had given her and swallowed some of the seeds. When Hermes delivered Persephone to her mother, Demeter was saddened to learn that Hades now had a permanent claim on her daughter. Yet, Persephone was allowed to remain with Demeter for eight months of a year even if she had to spend the other four in the underworld. This then was the reason why the earth was barren in winter—Demeter was sorrowing for her lost daughter.

DIONYSUS

As the god of the vine Dionysus was closely connected to the earth. Since his mother Semele was a mortal, Dionysus had the status of a demi-god. And like the grapevines that he established, Dionysus himself was dismembered and resurrected. He could inspire men with lofty visions or degrade them into raving savages through his powers of intoxication. His worship was marked by ecstatic ritual, by frenzied excesses in the wildernesses, and also by sublime dramatic festivals. He was often accompanied by the Maenads, or Bacchantes: wild women carrying rods tipped with pine cones.

When Dionysus' mother was destroyed by Zeus revealing himself in a flash of lightning, Zeus took her unborn infant and sewed it inside of his thigh. There the new god developed and had a second birth. But Hera held a grudge against the child and sent the Titans to tear him to pieces, which they did. He was brought back to life, however, by the Titaness Rhea, his grandmother. And Zeus saw to it that Dionysus was protected. Cared for by mountain nymphs, the god invented wine and in time he grew to maturity.

Then Dionysus set about his mission of establishing vine cultivation, with its mysteries and rites, throughout Asia Minor and India. He met opposition in various places but those who opposed him usually met with terrible fates. Accompanied by Maenads he visited Thebes, which was ruled by King Pentheus, his own cousin. Pentheus took an immediate dislike to this strange young man of dissolute appearance and to his enraptured retinue of women. He ordered the whole group chained and imprisoned, against the sound advice of Teiresias the seer. No earthly power could shackle the god and his followers; they escaped easily. Dionysus shattered Pentheus' palace and drove him mad. In his lunacy Pentheus decided to spy on the Maenads in their revels and went dressed as a woman. Out in the mountains he came upon the frenzied women as they feasted on animals they had torn apart. The Maenads rushed upon Pentheus, thinking him a wild beast. Pentheus' own mother ripped his head off while the others tore him limb from limb.

On another occasion Dionysus was walking along the shore and pirates captured him, seeing in the richly dressed young man an easy source of ransom. On board the ship the pirates tried to chain him, but their attempt was fruitless, for the shackles kept falling off. The helmsman recognized the divinity of the captive and pleaded with the captain to release the god, yet the captain spurned his advice. Then Dionysus caused the ship to run with wine and a vine to entangle the mast. Moreover, he changed himself into a lion and a bear, which terrified the crew. As Dionysus mauled the captain, the crew leapt overboard, except for the helmsman, and were transformed into dolphins. The god then resumed his true form and reassured the frightened helmsman that he had found favor with the son of Zeus and Semele.

Dionysus was never a great lover, but he did comfort the princess Ariadne after the hero Theseus had deserted her. In fact Ariadne bore him several children, and when she died he set the crown he had given her in the heavens as a token of his love for her. He was also faithful to the mother he had never seen. Determined to retrieve her from the underworld, Dionysus went down, forced Death to stand aside, and brought Semele out of that gloomy region. By virtue of his connection with Zeus he was able to secure a modest place for his mother on Olympus.

Commentary

The sources of these tales range from Homer to Ovid, a span of about eight hundred years. Yet these myths show a certain consistency. Most of them revolve around some conflict. The Greeks were contentious and loved fights, contests, battles of wit, trials. The Homeric epics, the Olympic games, the dialogs of Plato, the drama festivals, the public trials, and the recurrent warfare between Greek cities all bear witness to the prevalence of conflict in Greek culture. Of course conflict arises in any society, but the ancient Greeks made a way of life of it and created a dynamic but very unstable civilization.

In these myths of the gods we can locate the source of conflict in a keen sense of honor. The reason the Greeks accepted these diverse gods is that they behaved in ways similar to the Greeks. Although Olympian morality was almost nonexistent, the gods and goddesses possessed a very sharp sense of what was due them. The Greeks were a proud people, and they created gods and goddesses who lived by pride. Handsome, vigorous, immortal, these deities were exceedingly jealous of their own honor. A common theme of these myths was that mortals who infringed the rights of the gods suffered terrible punishments. Arachne, Actaeon, Teiresias, Anchises, Metaneira, Pentheus, and Adonis are cases in point. Another frequent theme was that disputes among the gods must be settled by arbitration. Poseidon and Athena, Apollo and Hermes, Aphrodite and Persephone, and Demeter and Hades had to settle their arguments in this way. And often one or both of the disputants were unhappy at the outcome. A heaven full of proud deities is just as unstable as a country in which pride is rampant. The only thing that held Olympus together, in fact, was the might of Zeus, who presided as supreme judge. Gods like these would have found the Sermon on the Mount unintelligible.

Three of the myths recounted in this section are vegetation myths. The story of Demeter is connected to the annual birth and death of grain, while that of Dionysus is related to the cycle of the vine. Unlike the other gods, both deities must undergo great suffering, Demeter through the loss of her daughter and Dionysus through his own dismemberment. Moreover, in each tale the underworld plays an important part. As the kingdom of Death it stands for the state to which every living thing must come. But the fact that Persephone and Dionysus are able to emerge from it, just as grain and grapes are reborn each year, holds out the hope of resurrection to mortals.

The third vegetation tale, that of Aphrodite and Adonis, is a restatement of the myth of Ishtar and Tammuz, which appears under "Babylonian Mythology." The Greeks tended to turn Ishtar's story into a parody of vegetation myths. The quarrel between Aphrodite and Persephone seems like little more than the wrangling of two matrons over a common lover.

Again we notice the ascription of personality to the gods. Generally the personality depends upon a god's functions. Thus it is natural that Poseidon be tempestuous as the god of the sea, or that Artemis be mannish as the goddess of the forest, or that Hermes be clever as a god of commerce and thievery, or that Aphrodite be seductive as the goddess of love, and so on. Yet while the gods gained in vividness and particularity from this process, they lost any transcendent quality they might have had and became almost parochial in their appeal. Once their characters, functions, and deeds had been defined, the Greek gods really could not develop anymore. For all their glamor they became lifeless stereotypes. And the end result was that people ceased to believe in them.

THE HEROES

PERSEUS

King Acrisius ruled Argos but possessed no heir who could take over the kingdom when he died. His only child was a lovely maiden, Danaë, but girls did not count for much then. Acrisius went to an oracle that informed him he would have no son, but that his own grandson would kill him. Greatly alarmed, the king had an underground chamber built, one with a skylight, and he imprisoned his daughter there in order that she might bear no children. However, Zeus saw the beautiful Danaë in her bronzed chamber and visited her in the form of a golden shower. Nine months later she gave birth to a son, Perseus. When Acrisius learned of this he hesitated to put them both directly to death, so instead he had his daughter and grandson sealed in a chest and cast adrift in the sea.

At length the chest landed on the beach of an island, where it was found and opened by a fisherman named Dictys. Being a kindly person, Dictys took the forlorn Danaë and her infant son home to his wife. The couple decided that they would care for Danaë and raise Perseus as if he were their own son, since they themselves were childless. Thus Perseus grew to manhood in congenial circumstances.

Danaë did not lose her beauty with the passing years, and Dictys' brother, the tyrannical king Polydectes, wished to make her his wife. But Polydectes regarded Perseus as a hindrance to his plans. Therefore he announced that he was going to marry another woman, which meant that everyone would have to present him with a gift. At the gift-giving feast Perseus was the only person present without anything to bestow upon the king. In his mortification Perseus rashly promised to bring the head of the Gorgon Medusa back as a gift. Polydectes was pleased, knowing that Perseus would die in the attempt, for one look from that hideous snake-headed monster turned men to stone. And even if Perseus should succeed, Polydectes would have a coveted trophy.

Perseus left the king's hall immediately and set sail for Greece, too upset to bid goodbye to his mother and foster parents. He went to Delphi to learn the whereabouts of the Gorgons, and while the oracle could not tell him it directed him to Dodona, the land of the whispering oaks. There Perseus learned nothing except that the gods were watching over him. Eventually though, Perseus met the god Hermes, who told him he must acquire some equipment from the Stygian nymphs. A pair of flying sandals, a magic wallet, and a helmet of invisibility would be essential for his success. Yet only the Graeae, or three gray women, knew the way to the Stygian nymphs. These crones lived far to the West beyond the river Ocean, and they had but one eye among the three of them. Hermes guided the young hero to them, and while one of the gray women was passing that single eye to another, Perseus jumped from behind and grabbed it. To get their eye back the Graeae told him where the Stygian nymphs lived. Again Hermes guided him there, and they borrowed the sandals, wallet, and helmet. In addition Hermes presented Perseus with a very sharp sickle with which to sever the Medusa's head.

Athena, too, proved helpful to Perseus, for she showed him how to distinguish between the three awful Gorgons, of whom only Medusa could be killed. The goddess also gave Perseus a mirror-like shield that would enable him to see the Gorgons without being instantly petrified. After this lengthy preparation, the hero was at last ready to take on the Medusa.

With his winged sandals he flew to the land of the Hyperboreans, and there he found the Gorgons sleeping. Gazing into his mirrored shield, Perseus approached them. As Athena guided his hand he struck off the monstrous head with one blow. From the blood of Medusa there sprang forth Pegasus, the winged horse, and a terrible warrior. Quickly Perseus put the head in his magic wallet and put on his helmet of invisibility. He did so in the nick of time, for immediately the other two Gorgons awoke. Seeing their slain sister, they set off to pursue and kill her murderer. But Perseus had no trouble eluding them, being able to fly without being seen.

He traveled south to Gibraltar and then east over Libya and Egypt. On the coast of Philistia he saw a beautiful, naked young woman chained to a rock. This was the princess Andromeda, who was awaiting execution at the hands of a sea-monster because her stupid, vain mother had claimed she was more lovely than the Nereids, or nymphs of the sea. Perseus fell in love with her and hastily arranged with her parents that if he could rescue her she would be his wife. When the monster appeared Perseus lopped its head off and freed Andromeda. Her parents, however, went back on their word, claiming that a previous suitor had a better right to their daughter. In addition, they summoned warriors to kill the hero. Since he found himself faced with too many enemies, Perseus drew the gory head from his wallet and transformed his antagonists to stone. Among them were Andromeda's parents, Cepheus and Cassiopia, who were turned into constellations for their treachery. But Perseus had acquired a wife.

He returned with her to the island where he had been raised and found that his mother, Danaë, and his guardian, Dictys, had fled to a temple for refuge from the courtship and vindictiveness of King Polydectes. Perseus went to the king's banquet hall to find Polydectes and his companions feasting. Greeted with insults, he pulled out the Medusa head as his gift for the king and changed Polydectes and the others into boulders.

To reward Athena for her aid Perseus gave her the head to wear on her breastplate, the aegis. And he returned the sandals, wallet, and helmet to the Stygian nymphs by means of Hermes. After making Dictys the new king of the island, Perseus set sail for his grandfather's kingdom of Argos, taking his mother and wife. He had hoped to be reconciled to King Acrisius, but the king no longer ruled there, having fled on learning that the grandson who was to kill him was a hero. Before long Perseus heard that the king of Larissa was going to hold an athletic competition, and he decided to enter. During the discus-throwing contest Perseus' discus was caught by the wind, which diverted it into the throng of spectators, where it killed an old man. The victim, of course, was King Acrisius, who had sealed Danaë and Perseus in a chest years before and cast them off to sea. Thus the oracle was fulfilled.

Stricken with guilt for killing a member of his family Perseus arranged to exchange kingdoms with an uncle, giving Argos for Tiryns. As a king he recaptured lost territories and fortified his city. And having settled down with Andromeda, he fathered a number of sons. Through these he became the ancestor of the great Heracles.

BELLEROPHON

Corinth was the location of Bellerophon's family. His grandfather Sisyphus, for informing on Zeus, was sentenced to roll a boulder up a hill forever in the underworld. His father, Glaucus, who fed human flesh to horses to make them savage, was trampled and devoured by those same horses at the will of Aphrodite. And Bellerophon himself had a luckless beginning. He murdered a fellow townsman named Bellerus, and by accident he killed his own brother.

He went into exile and arrived at the court of King Proetus. The wife of Proetus fell in love with the handsome young man and attempted to seduce him, but he rejected her advances. To retaliate she told her husband that Bellerophon had tried to rape her. King Proetus did not want to kill a guest, fearing the punishment of Zeus, so he sent Bellerophon to his father-in-law, King Iobates, with instructions that Bellerophon be put to death.

At Iobates' court Bellerophon was well received. After entertaining him as a guest, Iobates asked to see the sealed letter. Upon opening it Iobates was filled with the same consternation that had filled Proetus, for he too could not kill a guest. But as an expedient Iobates decided to send Bellerophon off on dangerous missions that were bound to finish him off.

Now Bellerophon had one consuming passion, which was to possess the winged horse, Pegasus, that had sprung from Medusa's blood. On sound advice he went to sleep in Athena's temple, and upon awakening he found a golden bridle beside him. With this bridle he went into the fields and discovered Pegasus drinking from a spring. Bellerophon had no trouble in putting the bridle on the horse and mounting it. In his suit of armor he and Pegasus glided through the air and performed marvelous stunts. With his new steed he felt ready to undertake any exploits that King Iobates had in mind.

His first task was to kill the Chimaera, a formidable fire-breathing monster with the front of a lion, the body of a goat, and the tail of a serpent. Bellerophon attacked the Chimaera from the air, riding Pegasus and shooting arrows at the monster. Finally he took a lance with a lump of lead on its end and held it to the beast's mouth. The flaming tongue melted the lead, which ran down in the belly and killed the Chimaera.

Iobates then sent Bellerophon against his enemies, the Solymi, but they were no match for Bellerophon's airborne assault with boulders. The king sent the hero against the Amazons as well, and he defeated them in the same manner. At his wit's end Iobates prepared an ambuscade for Bellerophon on his way home, and again he defeated the attack. Having failed to do away with the amazing young man, Iobates came to admire him for his valor and awarded Bellerophon his daughter for a wife.

However, his success did not last. After living in prosperity for several years Bellerophon decided that he belonged on Olympus for his famous deeds. Taking to Pegasus, he soared into the sky. But Zeus grew angry at this mortal's presumption and sent a gadfly to sting Pegasus under the tail. The horse bolted, throwing Bellerophon to the earth. Lame and cursed by the gods, the poor hero isolated himself completely from the company of men. Devoured by anguish, he wandered alone like a fugitive until he died. Zeus meanwhile had taken Pegasus into his own stable and used the wondrous horse to carry thunderbolts.

HERACLES

The most powerful and glorious hero of all was Heracles, better known by his Latin name as Hercules. A man of surpassing strength and coordination, he was able to perform superhuman feats. Yet it was small wonder because he was the son of Zeus, and Zeus had arranged that one day Heracles should become a god. A protector, friend, and adviser to men, he also performed services for the gods, helping them defeat the Giants and rescuing Prometheus from his punishment in the Caucasus. Heracles was honored throughout Greece, and in honor of athletic prowess he instituted the Olympic games.

The last mortal woman that Zeus ever slept with was Alcmene, the wife of Amphitryon, a woman renowned for her virtue, beauty, and wisdom. Zeus had selected her not for his own enjoyment primarily but because she was the aptest choice for bearing the greatest hero of all time. He wanted this last affair to be absolutely special. While Amphitryon was off fighting a battle, Zeus came to Alcmene disguised as her husband and lay with her for one very long night, regaling her in the meantime with stories of his victories. When the real Amphitryon arrived home shortly afterward he was surprised at his wife's lack of enthusiasm and her boredom when he recounted his military successes. She even seemed bored as he lay with her.

Nine months later Alcmene was about to give birth to twins. On the day on which Heracles should have been born, Zeus took a solemn oath that the descendant of Perseus born on that day would rule Greece. In a jealous fit Hera managed to delay Alcmene's delivery by magic and to induce an early delivery in a woman bearing another of Perseus' descendants. The result was that the infant Eurystheus was destined to rule Greece instead of Heracles. But Zeus in his anger made Hera agree that if Heracles should perform twelve tasks for Eurystheus he would become a god.

Alcmene gave birth to Heracles, the son of Zeus, and to Iphicles, the son of Amphitryon. When these twins were about a year old Hera sent two serpents to destroy Heracles in his crib. While Iphicles screamed and tried to escape, Heracles strangled the snakes, one in each hand. In his schooling Heracles preferred the athletic disciplines, over which he gained easy mastery, but he was never much of a thinker. Given to rash acts, he brained his music tutor with a lyre. After that Amphitryon sent him into the hills with shepherds. By the age of eighteen he had become the strongest man in the world as well as the ablest athlete, a hero possessed of great courage. Ordinarily a man of courtesy, he was prone to violent fits of temper under provocation, and sometimes he regretted his impulsive rages.

A lion was killing Amphitryon's cattle and Heracles went searching for it. On his first expedition he had the satisfaction of sleeping with King Thespius' fifty daughters with the father's consent. From these matings fifty-one sons were engendered. At length Heracles killed the lion. From it he made a cape and hood. In representations of him he was usually depicted wearing this lion-skin garment and holding the olivewood club with which he killed it.

The city of Thebes was forced to pay tribute to the Minyan king as reparation. Meeting the heralds who had come to collect this tribute, Heracles was treated with insolence so he cut off their ears, noses, and hands and sent them home. This precipitated a war in which the Minyans had the advantage. But with Athena's aid and his own reckless daring, Heracles helped the Thebans defeat their enemies. As a reward King Creon gave the hero his daughter Megara as a wife. But marriage did little to tame Heracles' rashness. Even the responsibility of raising sons could not curb him. So Hera sent a frenzied madness upon him in which he brutally slaughtered his children and wife. When he came to his senses he was overcome with horror and guilt. Despite the meager consolations held out by his friend Theseus and others, he contemplated suicide. Finally he went to the oracle at Delphi to learn how he could expiate his crime. The oracle informed him that he would have to submit himself to King Eurystheus of Mycenae as a slave and perform whatever tasks his royal cousin should command.

Although far inferior to Heracles in courage and might Eurystheus had cunning, and he devised a series of tasks that were next to impossible to complete. These were the "Twelve Labors of Heracles" that the hero undertook in his twelve years of servitude to the spiteful king.

His first labor was to kill the Nemean lion, an animal with an impenetrable hide. After vainly attacking it with arrows Heracles finally throttled the beast with his bare hands and carried it back to Mycenae. Eurystheus then resolved that Heracles must remain outside the city.

His second labor was to destroy the Lernaean Hydra, a serpent with nine heads and poisonous breath that lived in the swamps and ravaged crops and cattle. Having flushed the Hydra out of its lair Heracles attempted to club off its heads, but for every head that fell two grew in its place. With the help of his nephew Iolaus, who branded the severed necks, Heracles was able to kill the monster. He used the Hydra's blood to poison his arrows.

The third labor was to capture a deer with golden horns that lived on Mount Ceryneia and bring it back alive, an exploit that took Heracles a full year.

His fourth labor was to capture the wild boar of Erymanthus that was devastating nearby lands. On this expedition Heracles was treated hospitably by the Centaur Pholus, who opened a barrel of wine for him. But then other Centaurs savagely demanded it, and Heracles had to rout them with arrows. When he brought the boar back, Heracles showed it to Eurystheus, who was so terrified that he hid.

The fifth labor was to clean the Augean stables in one day. Since Augeas had thousands of cattle and their stables had not been cleaned for years the job seemed incredible, but Heracles diverted two rivers into the stalls that promptly cleaned the mess.

For his sixth labor Heracles was to drive away the enormous number of birds that were plaguing the people of Stymphalus. Athena helped drive the birds from their thickets and Heracles slew these flesh-eating birds with arrows.

The seventh labor involved capturing a maddened Cretan bull that Poseidon had given King Minos. Heracles mastered the animal and brought it back to Eurystheus.

His eighth labor was to capture the man-eating mares of Diomedes, which he could only accomplish by first killing their guardians and fighting off an army. He then served the horses' flesh to Diomedes. At this time he also rescued Queen Alcestis by fighting off Death when she was scheduled to die in her husband's place.

The ninth labor was to fetch the splendid girdle of Hippolyta, Queen of the Amazons. Hippolyta greeted Heracles cordially and agreed to part with the girdle. Hera, however, spread the rumor that the hero was going to abduct Hippolyta, so the Amazons seized their weapons. Thinking that the queen was behind the assault, Heracles killed her and many of the Amazons.

The tenth labor required stealing the cattle of Geryon, a triple-bodied monster on a Western isle. On his journey the hero set up the Pillars of Heracles to commemorate the trip. These were two enormous rocks, one of which was Gibraltar. Heracles slew Geryon, and after numerous difficulties he got the cattle home.

The eleventh labor consisted of getting the Golden Apples of the Hesperides. These were in a fabulous land far to the west, and they were guarded by goddesses. On his way Heracles met the gigantic bandit Antaeus, who forced strangers to wrestle with him and who gained great strength from contact with the ground. Heracles strangled him by holding him in the air. Finally the hero reached Atlas, the father of the Hesperides, who was holding up the sky. Atlas agreed to get the apples if Heracles would hold up the heavens in his place, and Heracles consented. Having fetched the golden apples Atlas decided to let Heracles hold up the sky forever. Heracles was dismayed and said he needed a cushion to ease the load, whereupon the stupid Atlas took back the burden and Heracles picked up the apples and sauntered off.

His twelfth labor involved bringing back Cerberus, the three-headed dog that guarded the entrance to the underworld. Hermes guided him into the netherworld, where Heracles rescued his friend Theseus from the Chair of Oblivion. He obtained permission to take Cerberus home, provided he used only his hands. Heracles attacked the monstrous dog, driving the wind from it, and forcibly led it back to Eurystheus, who bid him return the beast to Hades. With that deed his servitude to Eurystheus ended and his penitence for the murders of his wife and children was complete. In addition Heracles had earned the status of a demi-god, for he had fulfilled the requirement of Zeus.

Most heroes would have settled down after that, but not Heracles. King Eurytus was offering his daughter Iole to the man who could beat him in an archery contest. When Heracles won, Eurytus did not keep his word, and the hero vowed to get even. Moreover, Eurytus' eldest son, Iphitus, asked Heracles to help him find some stolen cattle. Enraged, Heracles slew Iphitus, and once again he had to consult the oracle at Delphi to learn how he might purge this crime. But this time the Delphic priestess refused to answer, so Heracles seized her tripod and threatened to set up his own oracle. Apollo became furious at this and would have fought with Heracles if Zeus hadn't intervened. Zeus made Heracles return the tripod and ordered that the priestess deliver an answer. She then told Heracles he had to be sold into slavery for three years and that his wages were to be paid to King Eurytus, the father of the murdered man.

Heracles submitted to his fate and was sold anonymously at auction to Queen Omphale of Lydia, who set the brawny hero to women's tasks. Nevertheless, Heracles fathered three sons on Omphale, rid her kingdom of bandits, captured a band of evil spirits, killed two murderous kings who forced strangers to work for them, and slew a gigantic serpent that was devastating the land. By this time Omphale had guessed the identity of her slave and she released him.

The hero was never one to forgive injuries. When King Laomedon refused to reward him for the rescue of his daughter Hesione, Heracles attacked Troy, killed Laomedon, and married Hesione off to his comrade Telamon. After receiving bad treatment from the inhabitants of the island of Cos, he sacked the place and slaughtered its king. Nor had he forgotten that King Augeas had never paid him for cleaning the stables. While laying Augeas' kingdom to waste, Heracles had to fight the Molionids, Poseidon's sons with one body, two heads, four arms, and four legs. No one managed to insult, cheat, or battle with Heracles and live.

His biggest grudge, however, was against King Eurytus, who had refused him his daughter Iole as the prize in an archery contest. Heracles had married Deianeira, and after accidentally killing her brother-in-law he was forced to flee. At a river crossing Heracles put his wife on the back of the Centaur Nessus. In midstream Nessus tried to violate Deianeira, so Heracles shot him with an arrow. But before Nessus died he gave Deianeira his blood as a love-charm to win Heracles' affection. At length Heracles set forth against Eurytus and killed him and his sons, taking the lovely Iole captive. Now Deianeira, realizing that Heracles loved Iole, soaked a shirt of his in Nessus' blood to win his love. And when Heracles put on the shirt he began to suffer a lingering, agonizing death, for of course Nessus had tricked Deianeira and achieved his revenge on the man who had slain him. Writhing with pain, Heracles grabbed a man and flung him into the sea. Then he began uprooting pines to build a funeral pyre for himself, and when it was completed he climbed upon it and ordered that fire be set to it. As the flames reached his body Heracles vanished in an apotheosis of lightning. And he was received into Olympus as the son of Zeus. There he married Hebe, the cupbearer, and enjoyed the life of the gods.

Commentary

In Perseus, Bellerophon, and Heracles we have three heroes renowned for monster-killing. Perseus slew the Gorgon Medusa; Bellerophon killed the Chimaera; and Heracles destroyed several monsters, including the Hydra. Yet each is distinct. Perseus is both elegant and impulsive, a man of loyalty to his family and friends, a dangerous foe to those who cross him, and a person blessed by the gods to perform one great deed. Bellerophon is violent and reckless, a killer who has the good luck to to tame Pegasus and thereby achieve all his successes. But the source of his triumphs is also the means of his downfall, for Pegasus throws him in attempting to reach Olympus. Heracles, too, is violent and reckless, but he has the grace to repent his wicked acts and to expiate them through arduous work. Lacking in real intelligence, Heracles must earn his heroism through sheer strength and skill. He is masculinity gone wild, begetting about eighty sons on various women, killing monsters, tyrants, and ordinary men alike, mastering savage creatures, and paying for his crimes with years of service.

One feature common to these stories is that each hero is obligated to some king when he performs his greatest acts. Perseus, Bellerophon, and Heracles gain their heroic laurels from necessity, because they are pledged to it and because their sense of honor demands it. Honor is naturally the driving force behind heroism, but it can also lead a man to rash criminal acts. Bellerophon ascending Olympus and Heracles killing Iphitus are examples of heroes violating the limits of human decency through pride. The Greeks were always aware of this double side to the hero, for it recurs many times in their myths.

JASON

King Athamas divorced his first wife to marry another. His second wife was ambitious for her own children and devised a way to get rid of Athamas' children by his previous wife. She arranged a famine that could only be alleviated by the death of her stepchildren. As these children were about to be sacrificed Hermes sent a golden ram to rescue them. This divine ram saved the boy Phrixus and his sister Helle and flew north with them. Helle lost her grip and fell into a body of water that was named the Hellespont after her. The ram delivered Phrixus to Colchis, where the boy was taken in by King Aeëtes. In thanksgiving for his deliverance Phrixus killed the golden ram as a sacrifice to Zeus, and its fleece was hung in a sacred grove.

Now the kingdom that Jason was supposed to inherit had been usurped by his cousin Pelias, and Jason was raised in secrecy for his own protection. Pelias had learned from an oracle that he himself would die because of a kinsman, and that he must beware of any stranger wearing a single sandal. When Jason arrived to claim rulership he wore but one sandal. A handsome, ambitious young man, Jason boldly confronted King Pelias and offered to let him have the wealth Pelias had accumulated, but that he, Jason, would take over the kingship. Pelias agreed but demanded that Jason fetch the Golden Fleece from far-off Colchis, thinking that the brash young man would never return.

Jason, consented to Pelias' condition and commissioned a ship, the *Argo,* to be built. He sent word to every court in Greece that he wanted volunteers, a band of Argonauts, to accompany him on his adventure. The journey would take them past Troy, up the Hellespont, through the Bosphorus, and all the way to the eastern shores of the Black Sea, where Colchis was located.

Among the many heroes who assembled for the expedition were Heracles, Castor and Polydeuces, Atalanta, Meleager, and Orpheus. The illustrious crew offered a sacrifice to Apollo before setting sail, and Jason himself was under the special protection of Hera.

The first stopover was at Lemnos, an island where the women had killed all but one of their males in a rage. But after a year without men the Lemnian women welcomed the Argonauts, slept with them, and gave them gifts of food, wine, and clothing. Soon thereafter the company lost Heracles when he went to search for his squire, Hylas, who had fallen into a fresh spring in his attraction to a nymph. Since Heracles did not return, the Argonauts had to sail without him.

The *Argo* slipped past Troy in darkness to avoid paying tribute to King Laomedon. A bit later Polydeuces had to kill King Amycus in a boxing match before the crew could continue on. Next the Argonauts came to a place where fierce birdlike females were plaguing a seer who had offended Zeus. These creatures, the Harpies, would swoop down at every meal to defile the seer's food, leaving it inedible. So two of Jason's comrades, both able to fly, pursued the Harpies. Moreover, they extracted a promise from Iris, the messenger of the gods, that the Harpies would never bother Phineus the seer again. In gratitude for ridding him of the Harpies Phineus foretold all that would happen to the Argonauts on the way to Colchis. And through his advice the heroes were able to pass between the Symplegades, or Clashing Rocks, without mishap.

Having gained the Black Sea, the *Argo* sailed along the southern coast toward the eastern shore. At one point the Argonauts were tempted to battle those savage warrior women, the Amazons, but they sailed on and at last came to the land of Colchis. The heroes put in at a secluded inlet and debated the best course to take. They decided to go directly to King Aeëtes and ask him for the Golden Fleece. Jason led some of his company to the palace, but they were greeted with hostility because the Colchians hated the Greeks. In fact King Aeëtes threatened to mutilate the Agronauts, but Jason answered him softly, promising to undertake any tasks he should set. Aeëtes then offered to give them the fleece if Jason could yoke two fire-breathing bulls, plow a huge field belonging to Ares, and sow the furrows with dragon's teeth. These seemed like impossible tasks to Jason, but he agreed to undertake them.

The goddess Hera had arranged that Aeëtes' beautiful daughter Medea should fall instantly in love with Jason. Not only was Medea lovely, she was skilled in sorcery. Medea contrived a meeting with Jason, who seemed entranced with her. He pledged to take her back to Greece with him and to remain faithful. In return Medea gave him an ointment that would enable him to conquer the bulls and plow the field. She also told him the secret of defeating the awesome crop of warriors that would sprout from the dragon's teeth. On the following day Jason yoked the fiery bulls, plowed the field, and sowed the teeth. When armed warriors sprang from the soil to attack him, Jason threw a stone into their midst and they fell upon one another murderously until not one was left alive. But King Aeëtes refused to give Jason the fleece, vowing to get rid of the Argonauts. Medea then bid Jason to take some men and steal the Golden Fleece from its place in the sacred grove of Ares. By night Medea led the troop to the grove, and there she charmed to sleep the dragon who guarded the fleece. Jason took the fleece from its perch and hurried back to his ship, the *Argo,* with Medea and his men.

Once on board the *Argo* Jason set sail. But before long they were pursued and cornered by the Colchian fleet, which was commanded by Medea's brother, Apsyrtus. To save Jason, Medea wrote her brother, saying that she had been abducted and that if he would meet her in a clandestine spot she would return the fleece and go home with him. When Apsyrtus met Medea that night Jason stepped out from hiding and slew him. Without Apsyrtus' leadership the Colchian fleet was dispersed, leaving Jason free to return home with Medea, who had become his mistress.

In another version of this story, Medea abducted her brother Apsyrtus aboard the *Argo* and there she murdered him. When King Aeëtes pursued the ship and drew dangerously close, Medea would cut part of her brother's corpse off and fling it into the sea. Aeëtes then had to retrieve the member to prevent his son's ghost from haunting him. In this way the *Argo* escaped the Colchian navy.

Jason and Medea had to purify themselves for the murder of Apsyrtus, so they journeyed to the sorceress Circe, who purged them. To get back to Greece the *Argo* had to pass between the cliff of Scylla and the whirlpool of Charybdis, but Hera saw that nymphs guided the ship. At Crete the Argonauts came upon Talus, a gigantic bronze warrior who threatened to sink the vessel with boulders. Again Medea came to the rescue, using sorcery to defeat Talus by calling upon the hounds of Hades. At length the Argonauts reached Greece and disbanded, returning to their separate homes.

When Jason arrived at Iolcos, his own birthplace, he learned that King Pelias had put his parents to death during his quest for the Golden Fleece. Medea offered to obtain revenge upon Pelias. Gaining an audience with the king and his daughters, Medea proclaimed her ability to rejuvenate men. Pelias, who was now old, grew interested. To prove her power she cut up an old ram, threw it into a boiling caldron, put in some magic herbs, and produced a frisky lamb. Medea then persuaded the daughters of Pelias to cut him up and put him in the pot. After they had done so, of course, Pelias was dead once and for all. Because of this mischief Jason and Medea were forced to leave Iolcos shortly. From there they went to Orchomenus, where they hung the Golden Fleece in the temple of Zeus.

The pair took up residence in Corinth, and Medea had two sons by Jason. However, Jason began casting his eyes about for a more suitable mate. As ambition would have it, he arranged to marry the king of Corinth's daughter, Glauce (also called Creüsa). When Medea learned of this she uttered some rash words that caused her to be banished from the city. Medea was heartsick at Jason's coldness after everything she had done for him, and she determined to take her revenge. Medea prepared a splendid garment for Jason's bride. When Glauce tried it on she felt her flesh burn away and died in agony. Knowing that life in exile would be harsh on her two sons, Medea killed the boys. She escaped Jason's wrath in a sky-borne chariot drawn by dragons. Jason also lost Hera's favor, and lived an empty life from then on. His single triumph was finished, and he ruled Corinth but produced no more children. Finally, one day as he was brooding under the prow of the *Argo* its beam fell on him, killing him.

THESEUS

Having no son, King Aegeus of Athens consulted the Delphic oracle, which told him in very obscure terms that he was not to lie with any woman until he reached his home, or he would die of grief. He failed to grasp the meaning, and while visiting King Pittheus at Troezen he got drunk, so Pittheus sent Aethra into him, knowing that this daughter would produce an heir to Aegeus' throne. Some claim that Poseidon also slept with Aethra on that night. In any case, Aegeus showed Aethra a rock under which he was leaving his sandals and sword, and he told her that if she gave birth to a boy and if he grew strong enough to lift the rock and recover the sword and sandals he should come to Athens to claim his inheritance.

In due time Aethra gave birth to Theseus, who grew up strong, athletic, courageous, and intelligent. On reaching manhood Theseus lifted the rock that his mother pointed out, reclaiming the sword and sandals. Now King Aegeus had left a ship by which Theseus might sail safely and easily from Troezen to Athens. But Theseus disdained the easy route, deciding to take the dangerous overland way, which was beset with robbers. Modeling himself upon his heroic cousin, Heracles, Theseus made a resolution not to attack anyone first but to mete out the punishment that fitted the offense. The bandits were rather inventive in their means of murdering travelers. One clubbed them to death with an iron cudgel. Another made them wash his feet and then kicked them off a cliff into the sea, where a man-eating turtle devoured them. And one bent two pines to the ground, tied his victims to the tops and released the trees. The most famous one, Procrustes, tied his victims to the bed, and where they were too long for the bed he cut off their limbs, but when they were too short he stretched them out. Theseus destroyed each of these killers by their own methods, clearing the way to Athens of robbers.

Upon arriving in Athens, Theseus was proclaimed as a hero. However, his father, King Aegeus, had taken in Medea after she escaped Jason, and had fathered sons by her. Medea immediately recognized Theseus as Aegeus' son, so she decided to destroy him in order that her own sons would inherit the throne. Telling Aegeus that Theseus was an evildoer sent by the king's enemies, she invited the new hero to the palace and prepared a poisoned goblet for him with Aegeus' consent. Just before Theseus drank from the cup he pulled his sword as if to cut meat. Aegeus immediately recognized the sword and knocked the goblet from his son's hand. The king rejoiced to find he had such a distinguished son, and Medea was forced to flee to Asia.

To punish Athens for the death of a son King Minos of Crete demanded a tribute of seven maidens and seven youths every nine years. These were to be given to the Minotaur to destroy, a monster with the head of a bull and the body of a man. The Minotaur lived in the Labyrinth, an incredibly complex maze from which it was almost impossible to escape.

The time had come for the tribute of youths and maidens to be paid. Theseus elected to join the party of doomed young people, hoping to destroy the monster and free Athens from King Minos' demands. Aegeus was distressed at the plan, yet he gave his son a black sail to be hoisted in case of disaster and a white one to use in case of victory. So Theseus set sail for the island of Crete.

Upon his arrival Ariadne, the daughter of Minos, fell in love with him and determined to aid him. From Daedalus, the man who constructed the Labyrinth, she obtained a thread by which Theseus could find his way out of the maze once he had entered. Armed with nothing but the thread, Theseus penetrated the Labyrinth with his fellow victims. At length he came upon the Minotaur asleep, and seizing his advantage he pounded the beast to death with his fists. By means of the thread he led his companions to freedom.

Having promised to marry Ariadne, Theseus took her as far as the island of Naxos and deserted her, either by design or by accident. One legend says he loved Phaedra now. He sailed for Athens, but forgot to take down the black sail and hoist the white one. His father, Aegeus, who was watching for the ship from a cliff, saw the black sail of defeat and hurled himself off into the sea in a fit of despair. Ever since then the sea has been called the Aegean.

Theseus then took over the government of Athens. Under his wise supervision a democracy was established, with town council meetings and a popular vote. Theseus himself held the position of commander in chief and allowed the citizens to run things as they wished in the belief that political liberty made people responsible and prosperous. On his own initiative he aided the unfortunate, forcing the city of Thebes to allow the burial of its dead enemies, befriending the blind and exiled Oedipus, and welcoming the bloodstained Heracles to Athens when no one else would have him.

Perhaps one reason Theseus set up a self-running form of government was that he found the cares of rulership oppressive, preferring to engage in heroic and risky exploits. He made an expedition to the land of the Amazons and brought their Queen Hippolyta back as his wife, begetting a son, Hippolytus, on her. The Amazons attacked Athens in turn. When their queen refused to return with them the Amazons, or warrior women, slew her. And Theseus then routed them from his country.

Theseus acquired a fast friend in an unusual manner, the reckless Pirithoüs, a fellow who stole Theseus' cattle to test his mettle. When Theseus pursued him Pirithoüs was filled with admiration for the hero and told him to choose the penalty he would inflict. At this Theseus felt an instant affection for him, and the two became close friends. Pirithoüs invited Theseus to to his wedding. As king of the Lapiths he also invited the savage horse-men, the Centaurs. These creatures proceeded to get drunk and one attempted to abduct Pirithoüs' bride, Hippodamia. In the ensuing fight both the lustful Centaur and Hippodamia were killed. A war followed between the Centaurs and the Lapiths in which Theseus took part. Their final exploit together was a masterpiece of impiety. Theseus decided to kidnap the child Helen and marry her when she grew up. Pirithoüs wanted to descend to the underworld and kidnap Persephone for his wife. So after abducting Helen, who was later recovered by her brothers, Castor and Polydeuces, the pair entered the netherworld to seize the goddess Persephone. Her husband, Hades, welcomed them and bid them sit down. When they did so Theseus and Pirithoüs could not arise again, for they had sat in the Chair of Oblivion and lost all memory of their purpose. Not until four years later, when Heracles harrowed Hell during his twelfth labor, was Theseus rescued from that fate and restored to the land of the living. But Heracles failed to rescue Pirithoüs, who had to remain in the den of Death.

Theseus' son Hippolytus grew to manhood as an expert huntsman in the service of Artemis. He had no use for women but delighted in his father's company. When Theseus took Phaedra as his wife, Hippolytus seemed to avoid his stepmother. Phaedra in turn grew madly in love with the elusive young man and tried to seduce him. When he rejected her Phaedra hanged herself after writing Theseus a letter accusing Hippolytus of rape. Despite his protests, however, Hippolytus could not convince his father of his innocence. Theseus prayed to the god Poseidon to kill his ingrate son. While Hippolytus was driving his chariot along a stretch of beach Poseidon sent a sea-bullock up from the water. The horses bolted in terror, throwing Hippolytus from the chariot. The fall killed him. In anger the goddess Artemis revealed the truth to Theseus, who became inconsolable.

As he grew older Theseus found little to take pleasure in. The Athenians had become extremely quarrelsome. And at last he died a miserable death at the hands of his host, King Lycomedes, who pushed him from a cliff because of a territorial dispute. Eventually the Athenians erected a tomb for their hero that would also serve as a sanctuary for defenseless persons.

Commentary

In Jason and Theseus we have two heroes who enjoy an outstanding beginning and must suffer a tragic middle age. It is interesting how the magical and the realistic combine in many heroic legends. Often a hero's success is due to supernatural aid. Jason could have accomplished nothing without Medea's sorcery and Hera's protection. Yet an actual personality reveals itself in the legend. Jason seems bland, obliging, competent, guided solely by ambition. An effective organizer, he supervises the *Argo* expedition, but the ultimate purpose of the quest for the fleece is merely to establish his right to rule Pelias' kingdom. It is a right that he never obtains, because Medea takes revenge upon Pelias and they have to leave Iolcos. He then determines to rule Corinth by marrying the king's daughter, a move that brings down Medea's wrath on his head. He gains Corinth but loses his own soul, in effect, and the same ambition that guides his one great adventure ruins him in the end. The legend for all its fantastic elements is psychologically truthful.

The same holds good for Theseus, who is a different type entirely. Whereas Jason is self-serving, Theseus' great exploits prove beneficial to others. In ridding the land route to Athens of robbers he makes the way safe for other travelers. In killing the Minotaur he frees Athens of its obligatory human sacrifices. In giving Athens a democratic government he makes citizens out of subjects. Theseus makes a point of defending the weak. He is one hero who consciously models himself upon another—the great Heracles. If he lacks Heracles' sheer masculine exuberance, he is more intelligent than his model and his deeds have more point to them.

Generous, brave, helpful, and intelligent, Theseus still has flaws that undermine his happiness and bring his life to a sad end. For one thing, he has a streak of rashness that harms him. In abandoning Ariadne he seems to lay a curse on all his marital attachments. He wreaks his son's destruction through angry ignorance. He nearly perishes when he goes down to the underworld to abduct Persephone. And his negligence in failing to hoist the white sail sends his father Aegeus hurtling from a cliff, a fact that may have determined the manner of his own death, since he too dies in such a fall.

The Greeks understood character in a way that other cultures failed to penetrate. They grasped how a trait like ambition could turn from a virtue into a bane, and how a noble personality might have serious defects that lead to ruin. They regarded the exploits of Jason and Theseus as worthy of emulation, but they also knew that a price had to be paid for heroism, and they did not flinch at showing that price in these legends.

MELEAGER

King Oeneus of Calydon married Althaea, but she lay with the god Ares and gave birth to Meleager. Shortly after the child was born the Fates visited Althaea, warning her that if a certain log on the fire was burned Meleager would die. Althaea hurried to rescue the log and stored it safely away. In time Meleager became an unbeatable warrior and an expert with the javelin.

King Oeneus neglected to honor Artemis one summer as he was sacrificing the first fruits of his harvest to the Olympians. To avenge herself Artemis sent a gigantic boar to ravage Calydon. The animal succeeded in destroying the crops and killing Oeneus' cattle and men. To rid himself of the boar Oeneus sent out word that he needed hunters to slay the beast, and that the one who triumphed would be rewarded with its tusks and pelt. Heroes showed up from many parts of Greece, among them Jason, Theseus, Nestor, Castor and Polydeuces. Yet one who turned up was a woman, Atalanta, who was as good at tracking and killing game as any man in the party. Artemis was her protectress. The goddess had sent the young huntress as a source of contention.

Atalanta had beauty, toughness, and competence. Her life had not been easy. When she was born her father exposed her on a mountain to die in his disappointment at not having a son. She had been nursed by a she-bear and raised by a family of hunters. Artemis had chosen well in sending her to the Calydonian boar hunt, for she proved a great source of trouble.

Although he had a wife, Meleager fell passionately in love with her. Atalanta was a woman after his own heart. Some of the hunters refused to join in the hunt because of her presence, but

Meleager managed to persuade them to stay. The group flushed the boar from its lair. Two men were killed in the onrush of the beast, and another died from a javelin that missed its mark. Atalanta struck the boar with an arrow, but Meleager finally killed it with two javelins.

In a gesture of gallantry Meleager awarded the pelt and tusks to Atalanta, who gladly accepted them. However, two of Meleager's uncles objected to this disgraceful act, since Atalanta had not killed the boar and because she was only a woman. In a rage Meleager killed the two uncles. But two other uncles raised a fighting force against Meleager, who killed them too. Meleager's mother, Althaea, became infuriated at the death of her brothers all because of a coarse, mannish girl. She took the log she had rescued from the fire years before and proceeded to burn it. Meleager felt himself devoured from within and died in agony.

Having obtained the trophies of the hunt, Atalanta went to her father's home to be reconciled to him, having proved herself the equal of men. Her father insisted that she marry, but Atalanta set the conditions. She would only marry a man who could beat her in a footrace. Since she was swifter than any young man, she could easily preserve her virginity. In addition, however, she would kill anyone who failed to beat her. A number of suitors died at her hands. But one Melanion requested help from Aphrodite, who gave him three golden apples and told him to roll each one in Atalanta's path as she gained on him. Aphrodite, after all, had no use for a woman who scorned to love. Atalanta looked stunning in her nudity, for in Greece races were run without clothes. Melanion, each time he saw Atalanta passing him, threw a golden apple in her way. She stopped to pick each one up, and in this manner Melanion won the race and gained her for his wife. Later Melanion persuaded her to make love in a place sacred to Zeus, and for this impiety Zeus changed the pair into lions.

ORPHEUS

The greatest mortal musician of all was Orpheus. The son of a Thracian prince and the Muse Calliope, he was beloved of

Apollo, who presented him with a wondrous lyre. Orpheus became a devotee of Dionysus and practiced the mysteries. He achieved vast skill on the lyre. Through the magical power of his music, rivers changed their courses, trees and wild beasts followed him enraptured, stones arranged themselves in a circle around him, and no mortal, divine, or natural force was immune to his enchantment.

Orpheus sailed on the *Argo* and performed prodigies with his music. The ship launched itself as he played. Quarrels were forgotten under his spell. Exhausted rowers gained new strength to his strains. Once Orpheus saved the life of every man aboard when his music lured the crew away from the fatal singing of the Sirens.

He fell in love with the wood nymph Eurydice, who agreed to marry him. On their wedding day Eurydice was pursued by Aristaeus, who had also become enamored of her. As she ran through a field a viper stung her as she stepped on it, and she died. Orpheus was heartstricken with grief, but he decided to go down to the underworld and persuade Hades and Persephone to release his bride. Taking his lyre, he charmed the watchdog of Hades to allow him to pass, melted the hearts of the Furies, and spellbound all the frightful powers of the netherworld. The king and queen of Hell were softened by his music, and they agreed to let him take Eurydice back to the land of the living, provided that he not look back along the way. Orpheus led his love back to the realm of light. As he stepped from the cavern of the underworld he anxiously glanced behind him, eager to see Eurydice. But he did so too quickly, for she had not yet emerged. She faded from his sight murmuring, "Farewell."

From that time forth Orpheus avoided inhabited places, keeping to the wilds of Thrace. He still played the lyre but he lacked the old enthusiasm. Orpheus took no other women, and for that reason the lecherous Maenads hated him. As he wandered in the forest one day, those frenzied worshipers of Dionysus swept upon him and tore him to pieces. They threw his head into a river, where it floated out to sea and came to the island of Lesbos, and there it uttered prophecies.

Commentary

The legends of Meleager and Orpheus show two heroes who become soft-headed over a woman and bring destruction upon themselves because of it. Meleager is a tough, skilled warrior; and although he is married, he falls passionately in love with the tomboyish Atalanta, killing his uncles because of her and thereby provoking his own death. Orpheus, on the other hand, is gentle, a dedicated musician who conceives a passion for Eurydice that lasts long after she dies, a love that calls the wrath of the Maenads down upon him. The Greeks regarded promiscuity in their heroes as permissible, but a headlong infatuation with one woman was dangerous, for it destroyed a man's prudence. Love was a form of intoxication that could ruin a hero.

A culture that stresses heroic values usually relegates women to an inferior position. To dedicate one's life to the memory of a woman, as Orpheus did, was considered unmanly. With Orpheus we see the end of the Greek heroic tradition, a poet-musician whom the Alexandrians elevated to the status of a hero. In contrast to him there are such ruthless, mannish heroines as Medea and Atalanta who seem to devour the men that lay claim to them. The soft man and the hard woman were generally unpleasant realities to the Greeks—the reverse image of their usual standards for the sexes.

The basic substance of the heroic legends is roughly the same material that our daily tabloids exploit: sex, violence, and wonders. Yet whereas these elements are presented randomly and without form in the tabloids, they have been given shape and meaning in the heroic legends. Frequently the hero is the man blessed by the gods to rid the world of some evil. He performs his feats without hesitation, and if he succumbs in the end his fame outlives him. Sex, violence, and wonders are his natural means of expression.

THE TRAGIC DYNASTIES

CRETE: THE HOUSE OF MINOS

There were two Cretan kings named Minos, the first being the father of the second. A son of Zeus and Europa, Minos I proved to be a progressive ruler, for under him Crete became the greatest naval power in the Mediterranean. He encouraged trade, constructed major public works, instituted an excellent legal code, established an educational system, and helped the arts to flourish. Through his wisdom Crete grew into an important civilization. His brother Rhadamanthus was also known for his just rulership, and when Minos I and Rhadamanthus died they were made judges in the netherworld.

Minos II was different from his father—proud and selfish. It was said of him that he pursued the maid Britomartis so relentlessly that she plunged to her death from a cliff rather than submit to him. Minos once offended Zeus, who decreed that any woman he lay with would die. However, he was cured by the exiled Procris, who fashioned a female model that drew off the poison in Minos as he lay with it. Minos took Pasiphaë as his queen and fathered several children on her, most of whom were badly fated. Thus Ariadne was deserted by Theseus; Phaedra committed suicide; Catreus was killed by his own son; Androgeus was killed by the bull of Marathon, which started the war with Athens; and Glaucus was drowned in a vat of honey, although the prophet Polyeidus brought him back to life with a magic herb.

The reason for these fatalities and misadventures lay with Minos. He had a knack for attracting disaster. In dedicating a temple to Poseidon he prayed to the god to send him a bull for sacrificial purposes. Poseidon rewarded him with a magnificent white bull, but Minos decided to keep it for himself and offer up another bull in its place. To punish this outrage Poseidon arranged that Pasiphaë, the wife of Minos, fall in love with the splendid bull. Pasiphaë confided her passion to the inventor Daedalus, who made a wooden cow to conceal her. In this manner the union was consummated, and Pasiphaë gave birth to the Minotaur, a beast with a man's body and the head of a bull. To conceal this monstrosity Minos had Daedalus build a huge palace with countless rooms and baffling passageways from which no one could escape. When this Labyrinth was completed Minos and his family and servants moved in, while the Minotaur was put in the nethermost region of the palace. Only Minos and Daedalus knew the key to this enormous place.

One day Minos received word from King Aegeus of Athens that Minos' son, Androgeus, had been killed by the bull of Marathon. Minos did not believe the report, suspecting political treachery. So he went on an expedition against Athens and its allies. In laying siege to the town of Megara, Minos attracted the love of Scylla, the daughter of King Nisus. Nisus was invulnerable because his life depended on a lock of purple hair above his forehead. However, Scylla, knowing the secret, betrayed her father and her city by cutting off the lock. Far from being grateful, Minos flew into a rage at the lovesick girl, who asked him to take her home with him. He punished Scylla by towing her through the water by her feet, which drowned her. Having conquered Megara, Minos attacked Athens and got the city to surrender. He then demanded a tribute of seven maids and seven youths to be sacrificed to the Minotaur every nine years.

When the next payment of human beings came due Minos took an instant dislike to young Theseus. He sent an undefeated giant of a boxer against Theseus, and the giant was trounced. Theseus offered the trophy of flowers to Ariadne, who fell in love with him and vowed to help him. She called upon Daedalus, who was an Athenian like Theseus. Having killed a nephew, an apprentice more skilled than he, in a rage of envy, Daedalus had had to flee to Crete. But he was homesick and resolved to aid his fellow townsman. He gave Theseus the thread by which to find his way out of the palace after destroying the Minotaur. In making his getaway Theseus set fire to the palace, sank a good portion of Minos' navy, and deserted Ariadne at Naxos. Minos was infuriated, knowing that Daedalus had helped Theseus, and he imprisoned the inventor and his son.

Daedalus fashioned a means of escape for himself and his boy Icarus—two pairs of wings made of a wooden frame and feathers glued with wax. The inventor instructed his son not to fly too high or the sun would melt the wax, or too low, for the water would destroy the wings. The pair then mounted the sky as Daedalus took the lead. Before they had gone very far Icarus became intoxicated with his new powers of flight and began to ascend to get a better view of the Aegean Sea. Unthinkingly he soared dangerously close to the sun, which melted the wax holding together the feathers, and Icarus plunged into the sea and drowned.

Eventually Daedalus found refuge with the king of Sicily, Cocalus. In his new place of exile Daedalus constructed an impregnable fortress. Meanwhile, Minos came searching for the traitor who had undermined him, arriving at last at Cocalus' court. He had brought a spiral shell of intricate design and he offered a reward to the one who could thread it. Cocalus took the shell and gave it to Daedalus, who threaded it by tying a string to an ant and putting it in the spiral maze. When Cocalus handed back the shell Minos knew he had found Daedalus and demanded the fugitive. Cocalus temporized. That evening when Minos was in his bath Cocalus' daughters poured boiling water on him and he died. The Cretans besieged Cocalus' fortress for several years but to no avail. Since all of Minos' sons had died before him, the Cretan throne passed to others.

Commentary

The stories of Minos II and Daedalus carry a strong element of poetic justice. When Minos withholds the sacred bull his wife become bestial, bringing scandal upon him. By killing Scylla, who betrayed her father and home for him, Minos seems to call down the betrayal of his own daughter, Ariadne, upon himself, not to mention her abandonment by Theseus. By requiring an unjust tribute of human beings from Athens he draws Theseus to his court, who kills the Minotaur, fires the palace, and sinks his ships. Daedalus must pay for killing his own nephew by becoming an exile, losing his only son and working for others as an honored slave. These are not coincidences but the fulfillment of a moral law by which sins are punished in kind. The Greeks knew that character determines its own calamities.

But these legends point to a larger reality than the merely personal. In them we see a condensed account of the rise and fall of Crete as a civilization. Early in this century when Sir Arthur Evans excavated at Cnossus he found a labyrinthine palace and ample evidence of a resplendent culture. Yet the legends of Crete show some grasp of how a culture grows and declines. Minos I is selfless, dedicated to producing a great civilization, and his personality is submerged in this effort. Under such a king a land is likely to prosper. Minos II, however, asserts his personality at the expense of Crete and his own family. He offends two major gods, leads his navy on missions of personal vengeance, builds a very costly palace for himself, and invites defeat by demanding a terrible tribute from Athens. Here we see Theseus from a different angle, not so much as the swashbuckling hero but as the instrument of Minos' humiliation and as an agent of Crete's decline. A king as selfish as Minos II seems likely to bring ruin to a small country with limited resources, and wealth and power tend to foster rulers like that. We have no way of knowing whether Crete deteriorated because of bad leadership, but these legends make it appear perfectly plausible. Kings with foolhardy arrogance could easily demoralize a people and weaken its will to resist invaders.

MYCENAE: THE HOUSE OF ATREUS

From its inception the dynasty of Atreus was cursed with pride and violence. The grandfather of Atreus was Tantalus, a son of Zeus who had the good fortune to banquet with the gods, dining on nectar and ambrosia. His first act of ingratitude was to take these divine foods and feed them to his mortal friends. The second was to steal the golden hound of Zeus and lie about it. But his third deed was an atrocity: he served up his own son, Pelops, as a feast for the gods, who recognized what was set before them and recoiled in horror. For these crimes Tantalus was sentenced to eternal torment in the netherworld. Famished and thirsty, he was set in a pool from which he could not drink and had a bough of fruits hung over him that he could not grasp.

Tantalus had a daughter, Niobe, who married Amphion, the King of Thebes, and bore him six handsome sons and six beautiful daughters. Extremely proud of her offspring, Niobe criticized Leto, the mother of Apollo and Artemis, for only having had two children. And when the women of Thebes offered incense to Leto to ward off punishment Niobe flew into a rage, declaring that she herself was more worthy of such offerings. The goddess Leto then sent Apollo to shoot down Niobe's sons and Artemis to shoot down her daughters. In anguish Niobe wept for her slain children, and Zeus changed her into a weeping statue.

After Tantalus had butchered his son Pelops to serve the gods, Zeus restored Pelops to life. But since his shoulder was missing, having been eaten by Demeter, Demeter gave him an ivory shoulder to replace it. Pelops became a favorite with Poseidon, although few human communities wanted him. In his wanderings Pelops came to Arcadia, which was ruled by King Oenomaus, who had a beautiful daughter, Hippodamia. When suitors came to woo her, Oenomaus would challenge them to a chariot race in which the loser would die. And because Oenomaus had the fastest horses in Greece Hippodamia's suitors had very short lives. However, she fell in love with Pelops and bribed her father's charioteer to sabotage Oenomaus' chariot. And Pelops received a pair of incredibly swift horses from Poseidon. Needless to say, Pelops won the race, killed Oenomaus, and married Hippodamia. But when the charioteer claimed his reward for undoing Oenomaus, Pelops killed him, and as the charioteer died he pronounced a curse on Pelops and his descendants. Nevertheless, Pelops had a very successful reign. He conquered the whole Peloponnesus, which was named after him, had many children, and celebrated the Olympian games in honor of Zeus.

Of his many sons Pelops loved the bastard Chrysippus the most, which made Hippodamia fear that her own children would lose the throne. When Chrysippus was murdered by Hippodamia two of her sons were implicated, so Atreus and Thyestes fled to Mycenae. Atreus acquired a golden fleece there, which would have established his right to rule. But Thyestes made love to Atreus' wife, Aerope, and obtained the fleece from her. Having been made king, Thyestes agreed that if the sun should move backward in its course Atreus could take over the throne. Zeus sent the sun backward across the sky, and Atreus acquired the kingdom of Mycenae. He had two sons by Aerope, Agamemnon and Menelaus. When Atreus learned that Thyestes had cuckolded him he invited Thyestes to a banquet and served his brother Thyestes' own sons, who had been butchered and boiled. Nauseated, Thyestes laid a curse on Atreus and his sons.

Thyestes then consulted the oracle at Delphi about how to get even. He was told to father a child on his own daughter Pelopia. So Thyestes ravished her in darkness, but she managed to get his sword. Having put Aerope away, Atreus went searching for a new wife and found Pelopia, who in time gave birth to Aegisthus. Thinking that the boy was his own, Atreus accepted him as his son.

A famine plagued Mycenae because of Atreus' revenge. It could be allayed only by Thyestes' return from exile, so Atreus sent for his brother, pretending reconciliation. When Thyestes arrived Atreus imprisoned him and sent Aegisthus to kill him. Thyestes recognized that Aegisthus' sword was his own, so he overpowered his son by Pelopia and bade him bring his mother. When Pelopia came to Thyestes' cell Thyestes revealed himself as her father and ravisher, whereupon Pelopia killed herself with the sword. Aegisthus then realized that Thyestes was his natural father, and in filial devotion he slew Atreus, who had raised him since infancy. Thyestes became the king of Mycenae again, while Atreus' sons, Agamemnon and Menelaus, went into exile.

The two brothers solicited the help of King Tyndareus of Sparta, who marched on Mycenae and restored Agamemnon to the throne of a rich and powerful state. By killing a cousin, Agamemnon acquired Clytemnestra, Tyndareus' daughter, as his wife. Menelaus married the beautiful Helen, and Tyndareus allowed him to rule Sparta. However, a Trojan prince named Paris abducted Helen, which precipitated the Trojan War. Agamemnon became the head of the Greek forces and left Mycenae for ten years to fight the Trojans. His wife Clytemnestra had little love for Agamemnon. He had killed her first husband, sacrificed their daughter Iphigenia to Artemis to allow the Greek fleet to sail, and taken a number of mistresses. To avenge herself Clytemnestra took her husband's arch-rival, Aegisthus, for her lover, and with him she plotted Agamemnon's death. When her husband returned victorious from Troy Clytemnestra greeted him warmly, although he had brought Cassandra, his foreign mistress, home with him. At the banquet given in honor of his homecoming, Aegisthus slaughtered Agamemnon as Clytemnestra murdered Cassandra. Aegisthus' forces were triumphant in defeating the king's supporters, and Aegisthus took over Mycenae and ruled it with Clytemnestra.

However, two of Clytemnestra's children by Agamemnon had been spared. The daughter Electra was allowed to live in the palace but was badly treated by her mother and Aegisthus. The son Orestes had been spirited away for his own safety. Raised at Crisa, Orestes made a friend of Pylades, the son of the king. Eight years later he went with Pylades to the Delphic oracle, which told him that he must avenge his father's murder or live as an outcast and leper. Returning secretly to Mycenae, he met his sister Electra at Agamemnon's grave. Electra welcomed him cordially, for here was the means by which Aegisthus and Clytemnestra would meet their just punishment. Orestes and Pylades went to the palace with news that Orestes was dead. Clytemnestra was delighted to learn of it and invited the pair in. Aegisthus heard the news and joined the queen, and Orestes slew him. Clytemnestra recognized her son and pleaded with him to spare her, but Orestes beheaded her according to the will of the gods. The Erinnyes, or Furies, made their appearance to punish Orestes with continual torment. Obsessed by guilt, Orestes returned to the Delphic oracle, where he learned that he must undergo a year's exile and then go to the temple of Athena at Athens.

His year in exile nearly unhinged his mind for good, because the Furies were relentless in their persecution of Orestes. At length he arrived in Athens and went to the temple, where he admitted his guilt, refusing to blame the gods for the deed. Apollo and Athena sided with Orestes against the Furies, who clamored for perpetual retribution. Athena spoke eloquently on Orestes' behalf and managed to persuade some of the Furies to quit tormenting him. But others were not satisfied with the gods' decision, holding that the old punishments were proper.

Still haunted by some of the Furies, Orestes returned to the Delphic oracle. It told him he must sail to the land of the

Taurians by the Black Sea, where he should seize the image of Artemis from her temple there and bring it back to Greece. This was a risky business, for the Taurians sacrificed all Greeks to Artemis. Orestes made the journey with his friend Pylades, and both were seized by the Taurians and taken to the Temple of Artemis to be sacrificed. The chief priestess was a Greek, and to the amazement of Orestes and Pylades she knew the family history. The priestess revealed herself as Orestes' long-lost sister, Iphigenia, who had been rescued from the altar at which Agamemnon was to kill her by Artemis. Carried to the land of the Taurians, she sacrified Greeks, just as the Greeks had been prepared to sacrifice her. Nonetheless, she disliked this practice and resolved to help her brother and his friend. On the pretext of taking them down to the sea to purge them of blood-guilt, Iphigenia made it possible for them to reach their ship with the image of Artemis. The group did not escape unnoticed, since the Taurians were in hot pursuit. The ship was stalled by a headwind, but just as the Taurians were about to get Orestes, Pylades, and Iphigenia, Athena appeared, caused the sea to calm, and ordered the Taurians to cease. The party sailed back to Greece, where Iphigenia performed the wedding of Pylades and Electra. Orestes could live in peace at last, having placated the Furies.

Commentary

The worst crime of which the Greeks could conceive was the murder of kin. From the time Tantalus butchered his son Pelops to Orestes' slaying of his mother this family was burdened with blood-guilt. The trouble is that each crime was done self-righteously, without the least remorse. Since blood must atone for blood according to the law of retribution, this dynasty nearly exterminated itself. The curses laid upon it were effective because of the streaks of violence and pride inherent in the family itself. Its members would scruple at nothing to obtain revenge. And yet Orestes managed to turn the tide even though he committed the most heinous sin of all in killing his mother. He did so by taking the full responsibility for his deed and by seeking to expiate it. Mercy was only permissible under these circumstances. The ancestors of Orestes right down to his parents were impervious to guilt, but guilt was absolutely necessary before mercy became effective.

The Greek tragedians, Aeschylus, Sophocles, and Euripides, each dealt with the story of Orestes as a means of exploring the problem of justice. According to the old Greek notion the only way to right a murder was with another murder. Honor demanded it. This concept was common to "shame cultures," in which justice was a matter of clan retaliation. But in civilized communities the notion was no longer adequate, and a "guilt culture" emerged whereby a man must pay for his sins in a court of law and be sentenced or acquitted. One had to take responsibility for one's deeds regardless of the motives that impelled them. In the legends of the House of Atreus we seek Greek civilization moving from a crude idea of justice to one that was impersonal and sublime.

THEBES: THE HOUSE OF CADMUS

When Europa disappeared, having been abducted by Zeus, her father, King Agenor, sent his sons to find and recover her, with instructions not to return unless they did. One of them, Cadmus, went to the oracle at Delphi to learn of Europa's whereabouts; but the oracle advised Cadmus to give up the search and, instead, to follow a cow till it fell from weariness and there build a city. Having followed the cow, Cadmus established the site of Thebes. He sent his companions to fetch water from a nearby spring that was guarded by a dragon. When the dragon killed a number of his companions Cadmus slew it. Athena appeared and told him to sow the dragon's teeth. After doing so, armed men sprang up ready to fight, so Cadmus threw a stone among them and they fell upon themselves until only five warriors remained, each of whom offered to serve Cadmus in building Thebes. However, Ares was angered at the killing of the dragon and forced Cadmus to serve him for eight years. Cadmus was then awarded the lovely Harmonia as his wife, and all the Olympians attended the wedding, bringing splendid gifts for the bride.

Cadmus ruled well, making Thebes a prosperous city. He and Harmonia lived to grow old peacefully, but their old age was troubled by terrible events. Having abdicated the throne in favor of his grandson, Pentheus, Cadmus emigrated from Thebes after Pentheus was slain by his mother in Dionysian madness. Cadmus' other daughters had unhappy fates, for Semele was blasted by Zeus; another leapt from a cliff holding her dead son; and a fourth had her son Actaeon torn to bits. Although some of these catastrophes were justifiable, unmerited suffering seemed to plague the House of Cadmus. Its founder was no exception. Sent abroad in their old age, Cadmus and Harmonia were changed into snakes before they died. Yet their death was favorable, for they went to the Blessed Isles.

Eventually Cadmus' great-grandson Laius became king at Thebes. Laius married Jocasta, but learned from the Delphic oracle that he would die by the hands of his own child. However, he got drunk one night and conceived a son. Laius and Jocasta exposed the infant on a mountain, riveting its ankles together. The child was found by a Corinthian peasant who took it to the childless King Polybus. Polybus accepted the boy and raised it as his own, naming it Oedipus.

As a young man Oedipus consulted the Delphic oracle, and it told him he would murder his father and marry his mother. Horrified, Oedipus did not return to Corinth, thinking that Polybus and his queen, Merope, were his true parents. Instead he went to Thebes, where a monster called the Sphinx was waylaying travelers and killing everyone who could not answer her riddle. The Sphinx had the body of a lion, the wings of an eagle, and the head and chest of a woman. When Oedipus confronted her she asked him what creature walks on four legs in the morning, two legs at noon, and three legs at evening. Oedipus answered, "Man," realizing the riddle referred to man's progress from infancy to old age. The Sphinx then killed herself, and the Thebans welcomed Oedipus as their king for having delivered them.

He married Queen Jocasta and fathered two sons and two daughters on her. Thebes flourished under King Oedipus. But then a plague struck the city, decimating the inhabitants. Pledged to aid the city, Oedipus sent his brother-in-law Creon to the Delphic oracle to learn how the plague might be stopped. The oracle said that the person who had killed King Laius years before must be caught and punished. Oedipus vowed to find the culprit and summoned the seer Teiresias to name the guilty one. At first Teiresias was silent, but goaded by the king he revealed that Oedipus himself was Laius' killer. Angered and dumbfounded, Oedipus inquired about the whereabouts of Laius' death, which had occurred near Delphi where three roads met. Oedipus recalled killing an arrogant old man and his retinue who had assaulted him in that very place. Of course it was Laius he had slain. Then a messenger arrived to tell Oedipus that King Polybus had died and left Oedipus the kingdom of Corinth. Presently the facts came out that Polybus was not Oedipus' real father and that Oedipus had been found exposed on a mountain. Jocasta grew distraught and pleaded with her husband to abandon his investigation. And at last the truth dawned on Oedipus that he had indeed murdered his father and married his mother. In despair Jocasta hanged herself, while Oedipus blinded himself in an agony of remorse. Wishing to be killed or exiled, he gave Thebes to Creon to rule as regent, and Creon promised to care for Oedipus' daughters.

Oedipus himself remained in Thebes for a few years, a blind and aging misfit cared for only by his daughters, Antigone and Ismene. After cursing his sons, Polyneices and Eteocles, for showing disrespect, Oedipus was exiled from Thebes by King Creon. Homeless and almost friendless, Oedipus was accompanied by Antigone, and at length the pair arrived at Colonus on the outskirts of Athens. There they were welcomed and taken in by Theseus. Just before he died Oedipus was told by the Delphic oracle that he would achieve the status of a demi-god and be a blessing to the land where he was buried.

Meanwhile, back in Thebes Oedipus' youngest son, Eteocles, had taken over the throne. His brother Polyneices had gone to the Argive court of King Adrastus to recruit an army against Thebes that would establish him as king. With the aid of Adrastus, Polyneices got five other captains and their troops to assault Thebes in an expedition known as "the Seven Against Thebes." One of these men, Amphiaraus, was a seer and knew that of the Seven only Adrastus would return alive. However, since Amphiaraus' wife settled family quarrels, Polyneices bribed her to send Amphiaraus against Thebes by giving her an ancestral necklace.

Having assembled his army, Polyneices marched on Thebes, sending a captain to attack each of Thebes's seven gates. Inside the city Teiresias told Creon that his son Menoeceus would have to die before Thebes could be saved. Creon, very disheartened, recommended that Menoeceus flee, but his son refused to dishonor himself, went into battle, and was killed. As the war dragged on most of Polyneices' supporters were killed, so Polyneices offered to settle the conflict in single combat with his brother Eteocles. The result was that Polyneices and Eteocles slew each other, thus ending the reason for the war. And as Amphiaraus had foreseen only King Adrastus escaped with his life.

Antigone and Ismene were appalled at their brothers' suicidal war. When it ended, Creon saw that Eteocles was given a hero's funeral, but he left Polyneices and the others who had made war on Thebes to rot on the ground without burial. This meant that their spirits had to wander on earth never at peace, specters to haunt the living. Furthermore, Creon ordered that anyone who should attempt to bury Polyneices or his companions would be put to death. Antigone, who had great family loyalty, was determined to bury her brother and lay his soul to rest, for she put divine law above kingly decrees. Ismene lacked the courage to aid Antigone. When Antigone had buried Polyneices, Creon had her walled up alive in a tomb. Teiresias the seer warned Creon that such an act would bring down the punishment of the gods. Creon then went to undo his mischief only to find that Antigone had killed herself with a sword. Now Creon's son Haemon was Antigone's fiancé, and when he saw his beloved dead Haemon killed himself, leaving Creon without progeny.

In the meantime Adrastus had gone to Athens to solicit the help of Theseus in getting Creon to bury his dead fellow warriors. Assisted by the mothers of the slain, Adrastus persuaded Theseus and the Athenians to march on Thebes. Their army gained the victory over the Thebans and reclaimed the corpses, which were given a heroes' funeral. Adrastus gave the oration eulogizing the dead, and the mothers of the slain were satisfied.

Ten years later the sons of the Seven, called the Epigoni, or After-Born, gathered to revenge themselves on Thebes. Teiresias foresaw disaster for the city, so the inhabitants fled during the night. The following morning the Epigoni entered Thebes, sacked it, and razed it to the ground. At the same time Teiresias died, the man who had been its seer for so many years.

Commentary

These legends deal with the founding, the hardships, and the fall of Thebes. As in the stories of Crete, the quality of leadership has a good deal to do with the fortunes of the city. And yet here we see a strain of innocence and unmerited suffering that the other tragic dynasties lack. Why Cadmus and Harmonia had such a hard old age, why Oedipus should unwittingly fulfill the horrid prophecy, and why Antigone and Haemon should die for serving the will of the gods are perplexing questions, for in each instance the misery seems unjustified or out of proportion to its causes. Sophocles, who dealt with the tales of Oedipus and Antigone in his tragic dramas, faced up to this problem squarely. In the end he can merely say that the ways of heaven are not man's ways, and that unmerited suffering is inexplicable by human standards. However, Sophocles still maintains his faith in the gods even it he can't understand them, but above all he maintains his faith in men, who can bear up under terrific agony and still retain their humanity. We see this most clearly in the legend of Oedipus' death and transfiguration, where Oedipus is granted a special dispensation from the gods after braving a merciless fate. Oedipus is a new kind of hero. If he is bold, resourceful, and intelligent, his outstanding trait is his ability to suffer. After blundering into a deadly trap set by the gods, he accepts the responsibility for the sins he committed in innocence by blinding himself and resigning his throne. He then undergoes long torment and at last emerges purified through his suffering. Antigone is also a new type of heroine, one who follows divine law and family duty at the expense of the state and who accepts death as her penalty. Only a race as unflinching and intellectually honest as the Greeks could have created or understood this family.

ATHENS: THE HOUSE OF ERICHTHONIUS

During the fifty-year reign of King Cecrops of Athens the famous contest took place between Poseidon and Athena for possession of the city. According to one version Cecrops let the Athenians vote on which deity had given the city the best gift, Athena with her olive tree or Poseidon with his salt-water well. The men sided with Poseidon, but the women supported Athena, who won. Poseidon then flooded the countryside, and the men decided to deprive the women of the vote to appease him.

It was also in Cecrops' reign that Hephaestus scuffled with Athena, spilled his seed on the earth, and produced Erichthonius, whom Athena placed in a chest and gave to Cecrops' three daughters, warning them not to open the chest. The young women lifted the lid and saw an infant with writhing serpents for legs. This alone should not have surprised them, for their father Cecrops was a dragon from the waist down. But Athena drove the disobedient girls mad and they leapt from the Acropolis to their deaths. Under the protection of Athena, Erichthonius grew to manhood and assumed the Athenian throne. When he died his son Pandion reigned.

King Pandion had two daughters, Procne and Philomela. The king of Thrace, Tereus, took Procne as his wife and she gave him a son, Itys. An oracle declared that Itys would be killed by a blood relative, so Tereus slew his own brother in a rage of suspicion. Now Tereus fell in love with his wife's sister, Philomela. To get Procne out of the way he cut out her tongue, rendering her speechless, and put her in the slave quarters. Tereus then went back to Athens and told King Pandion that Procne had died. So Pandion gave him Philomela to marry, but Tereus raped her before the wedding. Procne wove a bridal robe for her sister that told where she was, and Philomela came to her aid. Both women hated Tereus, but it was Procne who killed her son Itys and sent the boiled flesh to Tereus for his dinner. On learning what he had eaten Tereus was dumbstruck. Then he seized an axe to pursue the fleeing sisters. Just as he was about to hack them to bits the gods changed the three of them into birds: Procne into a swallow, Philomela into a nightingale, and Tereus into a hoopoe or a hawk. When King Pandion heard he had lost both of his daughters he died of grief, and Athens went to his son Erechtheus.

But Erechtheus, too, had children fated to misfortune. One of his daughters, Orithyia, was courted by Boreas, the North Wind. Erechtheus did not approve of this blustering suitor, and he was rejected. Not to be thwarted, Boreas abducted Orithyia in a gust that carried her off to the North, where he ravished her. In time Orithyia gave birth to two sons that were to sail with Jason on the *Argo*.

Another of Erechtheus' daughters, Procris, married Cephalus, a man with a passion for hunting. He went off on a long expedition to hunt and Eos, the goddess of the dawn, fell in love with him. When she failed to seduce him Eos told Cephalus that surely his wife Procris had been unfaithful to him during his absence. To test his wife's fidelity Cephalus disguised himself, returned home and tried to tempt Procris. Although she never gave in to this stranger she softened considerably, and Cephalus revealed his true identity in a rage. Just as angry, Procis left him and went to Crete, where she cured Minos of a curse that Zeus had inflicted on him. In gratitude Minos gave her a spear that never missed its mark. Eventually Cephalus sought Procris out, having repented of his jealous fit, and the two were reconciled. As a token of her love Procris gave her husband the magic spear, and he took her with him on his next hunting trip. Seeing something move in the thicket before him, Cephalus hurled the spear, killing the only woman for whom he cared.

A third daughter of Erechtheus, Creüsa, was ravished by Apollo against her will and secretly gave birth to a son in a cave, where she abandoned it, fearing for her own safety. Erechtheus married her off to a foreign ally of his, a man named Xuthus. Creüsa produced no children to Xuthus, who desperately wanted a son. He finally took Creüsa with him to Apollo's oracle at Delphi. The oracle told him that the first boy he met on leaving the temple would be his. He found Creüsa talking to Ion, a lad who served Apollo at the temple. Xuthus joyfully greeted the boy and claimed him as his son, thinking he must have sired Ion on a Maenad, whereas Apollo had simply intended the boy as a gift. Creüsa felt a deep bitterness at this, because Xuthus now had a son while she had lost hers for good. She also hated Apollo for having raped and deserted her. Outraged, Creüsa tried to poison Ion, but when her attempt was discovered, Ion and a crowd were about to kill her. But then the Delphic priestess brought forth the blanket in which Ion had been wrapped as an infant, and Creüsa recognized it as her own. Creüsa embraced Ion as her son, but the priestess warned against telling Xuthus the truth. Presently Athena appeared at Apollo's request and prophesied that Ion would one day rule Athens. Creüsa gave up the long grudge she had felt for Apollo, and through her son she lost her dislike of men in general.

Another version says that Erichthonius and Erechtheus were the same person and that he had snakes for legs which so frightened the daughters of Cecrops that they leapt from the Acropolis. But Erechtheus himself had daughters who ended unhappily. Orithyia was abducted and raped by the North Wind. When Erechtheus as king of Athens made war on the Eleusinians, the foe called in Eumolpus, the son of Poseidon, to help them. Erechtheus learned from the oracle that he would win if his daughters perished. Since their father refused to kill them, they sacrificed themselves by jumping from the Acropolis, which allowed Erechtheus to win. However, for killing Eumolpus, Erechtheus was slain by Poseidon, and his son Pandion became king.

In a variant to the tale of Tereus, Pandion married off his daughter Procne to the Thracian king Tereus in order to gain an ally. Procne was lonely in Thrace, so she invited her sister Philomela to visit. When the girl arrived, Tereus raped her and cut out her tongue to keep her from telling his wife. But Procne learned the truth from a tapestry woven by Philomela in the women's quarters. She took revenge on her husband by serving him their son Itys for dinner. And after telling him of it, she and Philomela made their escape. In time Tereus caught up with the pair and was about to kill them, but the gods turned the three of them into birds: Philomela into the silent swallow, Procne into the nightingale that mourns, "Tereus, Tereus, Itys, Itys," and Tereus into the hoopoe that calls, "Where? Where?"

Commentary

Each of the tragic dynasties has a dominant theme. In that of Minos it is the use of power and retribution for wrong. In that of

Atreus it is kin murder and atoning for this family curse. In that of Cadmus it is unmerited suffering and the fortitude necessary to overcome it. And here, with the House of Erichthonius, it is the battle of the sexes, in which rape is a major motif.

These legends present the relationships between men and women as soured, thorny, fated to unhappiness. The contest between Poseidon and Athena for possession of Athens triggers a conflict between the Athenian men and women in which the women lose their voting rights. This fight sets the stage for the other legends. Appropriately, the founder of the Athenian dynasty, Erichthonius, is engendered when Hephaestus tries to rape Athena.

In the tale of Procne the battle of the sexes becomes a murderous war, with ferocity and ruthless lust on Tereus' part and a hate-ridden urge for revenge on that of Procne and Philomela. With the story of Procris it is Cephalus' unbalanced jealousy and Procris' pride that breaks up their marriage. The happy reunion is destroyed when Procris' gift to Cephalus becomes the instrument that kills her. While Orithyia is kidnaped and ravished by Boreas, her sister Creüsa is raped and abandoned by Apollo. Creüsa has a barren marriage to Xuthus. It takes a miraculous intervention on the part of Athena and the Delphic priestess to reconcile Creüsa to men and to Apollo. The flaws of these characters are those of normal human beings—pride, lust, wrath, jealousy, selfishness, and so on—but in this dynasty they are magnified beyond their normal limits. The House of Erichthonius seems afflicted with a lack of balance that tends to disturb or ruin its marriages. Despite the fabulous elements in these legends, there is a core of realism that is based on an understanding of human character.

It is interesting that each of the tragic dynasties has its own individuality. This may be due to prominent traits in the Cretans, Mycenaeans, Thebans, or Athenians that distinguished them from each other. It may be that there were actually dynasties with those qualities. Or it may be that a certain kind of story tended to evolve around a group of legendary figures. Of course, the conscious literary artistry of the Greek writers would have accentuated this shaping process, particularly with the tragic dramatists. But the important thing is that personality flaws often run in families, and that these defects do affect the destiny of a family. In Greek mythology the dictum that "character is fate" applies as much to clans as it does to individual heroes.

THE TROJAN WAR

THE PRELIMINARIES

King Priam ruled in the wealthy, fortified city of Troy. He was not only prosperous, but he had fifty or more children, and it seemed as if good fortune would bless him and his children for a long time to come. However, his wife, Hecuba, had a nightmare in which she gave birth to a deadly firebrand. The seers interpreted this to mean that her unborn child would destroy Troy and its inhabitants. When the infant was born it was exposed on Mount Ida, but a she-bear nursed it and it survived, growing up as a shepherd called Alexander, or Paris. Paris took the nymph Oenone as a lover.

At the wedding of Peleus and Thetis the gods were enjoying themselves when Eris, or Strife, threw a golden apple into their midst with the words, "For the fairest," attached. Hera, Athena, and Aphrodite all claimed the apple and asked Zeus to judge between them, but he wisely refused, directing the three goddesses to a shepherd on Mount Ida who could decide the loveliest. The goddesses approached Paris and each offered Paris a bribe for selecting her. Hera promised to make him a king who would rule Asia and have great wealth. Athena offered to give him wisdom and an invincible valor in warfare. But Aphrodite won the apple by promising Paris the most beautiful woman in the world—the spectacular Helen. His choice was imprudent to say the least, since he made implacable enemies of Hera and Athena, both of whom vowed to destroy him and Troy.

On learning that he would possess Helen, Paris first went to Troy and established himself as a true prince, the legitimate son of Priam and Hecuba. He now had no further use for Oenone and abandoned her. Then he sailed for Sparta, where he seduced

Helen during her husband's absence and took her back to Troy with him.

Meanwhile Paris' sister Cassandra was faced with trouble. Apollo gave her the gift of prophecy while trying to make love to her, but she had taken a vow of chastity and resisted him. In anger Apollo turned his gift into a curse by making it so that no one would believe her. When Paris returned with Helen and stood before Priam to get his father's acceptance Cassandra came into the room, visualized all that would occur because of Paris and his lust, gave shrieks of despair, and railed at her immoral brother. Thinking Cassandra mad, Priam had his daughter locked in a palace cell.

When Menelaus returned to Sparta and found his wife Helen gone, he summoned the Greek leaders to go with him to conquer Troy and recover Helen. These leaders were pledged to aid Menelaus, for as they had courted Helen too they had taken an oath to avenge any dishonor that fell upon her future husband because of her. Thus Paris precipitated the Trojan War, which would fulfill the prophetic dream his mother had of giving birth to a firebrand that would destroy Troy.

The Greek chieftains assembled at Aulis under the leadership of Agamemnon, the brother of Menelaus. Most of the warriors were glad to go, eager to burn and sack Troy. But two heroes were reluctant. An oracle told Odysseus that he would be twenty years from home if he went, so he feigned madness when the Greek leaders came for him. Palamedes exposed the ruse, and Odysseus had to go. Since Troy could not be taken without the help of Achilles, the Greeks went to Scyros to fetch him. Achilles was practically invulnerable as a fighter, for his mother, the nymph Thetis, had dipped him in the River Styx at birth, rendering him immortal everywhere but in his heel, where she had held him. Tutored by Chiron, he became an incredibly swift and fearsome warrior. Knowing he would have a short but glorious life if he went to Troy, Thetis disguised her valiant son in women's clothing at the Scyrian court. However, Odysseus discovered Achilles by a trick, and he too consented to go.

At first the Greeks sailed to Mysia, and believing it to be Troy they made war. The Mysian king, Telephus, was wounded in the battle by Achilles. Learning of their error, the Greeks sailed back to Aulis. Since an oracle had said that Troy could not be taken without Telephus' advice, Achilles was obliged to heal his victim. The renegade Trojan prophet, Calchas, had sided with the Greeks, and when unfavorable winds prevented the Greeks from sailing, Calchas declared that the goddess Artemis wanted the sacrifice of a virgin. Agamemnon's daughter Iphigenia was chosen and sent for under the pretext that she would marry Achilles. Yet she willingly allowed herself to be sacrificed for the Greek cause. Some say, though, that Artemis put a deer in her place and carried her off to the land of the Taurians. In any case the Greek expedition was able to reach Troy.

THE COURSE OF THE WAR

An oracle had said that the first to leap ashore on Trojan territory would be the first to die. Protesilaus took this burden on himself and was greatly honored for it after being slain in a skirmish with Hector, the Trojan prince. A mighty warrior, Hector was the mainstay of Troy in the ten years of fighting that followed. Yet Hector bore the knowledge that both he and his city were doomed. If his brother Troilus had lived to be twenty Troy might have been spared, but Achilles slew the boy in his teens. Troy had one other defender of note, Aeneas, an ally from a neighboring land. The Greek army, however, was full of heroes. In addition to Agamemnon, Menelaus, Nestor, Odysseus, and Achilles, there were Diomedes and the two Ajaxes.

The gods took part in the war as well, affecting the outcome of various battles. Apollo, Artemis, Ares, and Aphrodite sided with the Trojans, while Hera, Athena, Poseidon, Hermes, and Hephaestus aided the Greeks. Zeus might interfere on occasion, but he maintained neutrality for the most part, being fully aware of what would happen.

After nine years of fighting the Greeks had managed to lay waste many kingdoms allied to Troy in Asia Minor, but they had not made much headway against Troy itself. There was friction in the Greek camp. Odysseus still bore a grudge against Palamedes, the man who had ruthlessly shown his madness to be a hoax. When Palamedes denounced Odysseus for an unsuccessful foraging expedition, Odysseus framed Palamedes, making him appear a traitor. Palamedes was stoned to death as a result.

But then a more disastrous quarrel broke out, this time between Agamemnon and Achilles. Agamemnon had taken the daughter of a priest of Apollo as a trophy of war, and when her father came to ransom her Agamemnon sent him off without her. The priest called upon Apollo to avenge him, so Apollo sent a plague to the Greeks that killed many. Achilles called a council and demanded that Agamemnon give back the girl, Chryseis. Agamemnon angrily agreed, but he insisted on taking Achilles' own prize, the maid Briseis, in her place. It would have come to murder had not Athena intervened. Achilles then gave up Briseis, but in his wounded pride he decided to withdraw from the war. Since the Greek victories up to that point had been due to Achilles' prowess, this was a calamity for the Greeks. Achilles told his mother Thetis to petition Zeus for Trojan victories, which she did.

Quick to see that Achilles and his band of Myrmidons had retired from the fighting, the Trojans made a spirited attack. Agamemnon then granted a truce in which it was agreed that Paris and Menelaus should fight in single combat for Helen. But the duel was inconclusive, for Aphrodite, seeing that Paris was losing, wrapped him in a magic cloud and took him back to Troy. Menelaus searched for Paris in the Trojan ranks, and Agamemnon demanded that the Trojans surrender Helen. The Trojans were willing, which might have ended the war. But Hera wanted Troy devastated, so she dispatched Athena to break the truce. Athena then persuaded the Trojan archer Pandarus to fire an arrow at Menelaus. The shot grazed Menelaus, and the fighting resumed in an angry turmoil.

The greater Ajax and Diomedes fought in an inspired manner, killing Trojans by the score. Diomedes slew Pandarus and wounded Aeneas. Aphrodite came to rescue her son Aeneas, but Diomedes wounded her in the wrist, causing the goddess to flee. However, Apollo bore Aeneas from the field and Artemis cured him. Diomedes then encountered Hector, who was accompanied by the bloody Ares, god of battle. Diomedes was intimidated and the Greeks drew back, but Athena gave Diomedes the courage to attack Ares. Injured, Ares bellowed in pain and fled to Olympus.

Forced to retreat, Hector was advised to return to Troy and bid his mother Hecuba to offer her most beautiful robe with a plea for mercy to the hostile Athena. Yet this gesture failed to placate the goddess. After a poignant conversation with his wife Andromache and dandling his infant son Astyanax, Hector went back to the field and issued a challenge to duel to Achilles, who declined. Ajax took up the challenge, and in the fight Ajax slightly bested Hector. The two warriors parted after exchanging gifts.

Honoring his promise to Thetis, who had asked him to aid the Trojans, Zeus ordered the other gods from the battlefield. As a consequence the Greeks lost badly. Under Hector's pounding assault the Greeks were almost driven back to their ships by evening. Disheartened, Agamemnon considered abandoning the siege of Troy. But Nestor, who was old and wise, recommended that he make peace with Achilles by giving him back Briseis and a pile of wealth to boot. Achilles received the deputation from Agamemnon courteously, but refused the offer. His pride was at stake, and he would only fight if he or his Myrmidons were threatened. The situation seemed hopeless. Yet that night Odysseus and Diomedes made a raid on the Trojan camp, killing many, including King Rhesus, and stealing some horses.

The next day the Greeks were forced back to the beach, and Agamemnon, Odysseus, and Diomedes were wounded. Hera resolved to turn the tide of battle. Using Aphrodite's magic girdle, she seduced Zeus into making love to her and forgetting about the war. While Zeus was engaged Poseidon entered the fray and made the Trojans retreat. Ajax hurled a boulder at Hector and felled him, whereupon the Trojans ran madly for the city. Zeus recovered from his infatuation, saw the rout, threatened to beat Hera, and ordered Poseidon from the field.

Apollo came to Hector's aid, breathing vigor into him. Once again the Trojans gained the upper hand. With Hector in the forefront the Trojans smashed down the protective barricades the Greeks had built to protect their ships. Greatly alarmed, Achilles' companion Patroclus tried to persuade his friend to fight, but still Achilles declined. Patroclus then borrowed Achilles' armor and entered the battle. Thinking that Achilles was now fighting, the Trojans panicked as Patroclus slaughtered them right and left. He made his way to the walls of Troy, but Apollo dazed him as he tried to scale them. Hector found Patroclus then and slew him, stripping him of his splendid armor.

When Achilles received news of Patroclus' death he threw himself on the ground in a frenzy of grief and had to be restrained. His mother, Thetis, brought him new armor fashioned by Hephaestus, but she warned him that if he killed Hector he himself would perish soon after. Nevertheless, Achilles was determined to slay Hector and a host of Trojans besides. The next morning he made a formal reconciliation with Agamemnon and began fighting immediately.

The clash of arms that day was terrible. While Hector and Aeneas killed many Greeks they could not stop Achilles in his furor of bloodletting. In fact, both Aeneas and Hector had to be rescued with divine help. Achilles filled the Scamander River so full of bodies in his dreadful onslaught that the waters overflowed and nearly drowned him. The gods, too, engaged in battle among themselves, as Athena felled Ares, Hera boxed Artemis' ears, and Poseidon provoked Apollo.

Eventually Achilles encountered Hector outside the walls of Troy. Hector ran from his opponent in a lapse of courage, circling the city three times. But Athena duped him into making a stand, and Achilles' lance caught him in the throat. Although Hector had pleaded with Achilles to let his parents ransom his body as he died, Achilles denied him jeeringly. Then Achilles took Hector's corpse, tied it behind his chariot, and dragged it back to the Greek camp as Hector's wife watched from the walls of Troy.

Since Patroclus' ghost demanded burial, Achilles prepared a glorious funeral. He cut the throats of twelve Trojan nobles as a sacrifice on Patroclus' pyre, and funeral contests in athletics followed. For eleven days Achilles dragged Hector's body around the pyre, yet Apollo preserved the corpse from corruption. Then Zeus directed Thetis to bid Achilles accept the ransom offered by King Priam for Hector's body. Zeus also sent Hermes to Priam, and Hermes guided the old king with his ransom through the Greek lines to Achilles' camp. Achilles treated Priam with courtesy, for Priam reminded him of his own aged father, Peleus. Achilles took Hector's weight in gold and gave Priam the body, which Priam took back to Troy. During the next eleven days there was a truce as the Trojans mourned for the dead Hector, whom they cremated and buried.

Achilles managed to kill the Amazon Queen, Penthesileia, in the battles that followed. And when the Trojans brought in Ethiopian reinforcements under Prince Memnon, things went hard with the Greeks, for many were slain. But when Memnon killed Achilles' friend Antilochus, Achilles retaliated by killing Memnon in a duel. However, Achilles' life was drawing to a close, as he well knew. One day in battle Paris shot at Achilles, and the arrow, guided by Apollo, struck him in the right heel, the only place where he was vulnerable. The Greeks had a difficult time retrieving his corpse from the field. Only the efforts of Ajax and Odysseus saved Achilles' body from the Trojans. The hero was given a magnificent funeral.

There arose a dispute as to whether Ajax or Odysseus should receive Achilles' resplendent armor. The Greek commanders voted on it and awarded the armor to Odysseus. Dishonored and furious, Ajax resolved to kill a number of Greek leaders, including Odysseus. But Athena visited him with madness, and that night Ajax butchered a number of cattle under the delusion that they were the men who had slighted him. When Athena removed his frenzy Ajax saw his irremediable folly and committed suicide out of shame.

THE FALL OF TROY

With their two most valiant warriors dead the Greeks became anxious about ever taking Troy. Force of arms had been unsuccessful, so they turned to oracles increasingly. Calchas told them they needed the bow and arrows of Heracles to win the war. These items were in the hands of Prince Philoctetes, a warrior the Greeks had abandoned years before on the way to Troy at the island of Lemnos because of a loathsome wound that would not heal. Odysseus and Diomedes were dispatched to fetch the weapons. On Lemnos, Odysseus tricked Philoctetes into handing over the bow and arrows and prepared to leave, but Diomedes offered to take Philoctetes back to Troy with them, where he would be cured of his wound. Philoctetes swallowed his long bitterness, sailed for Troy, and killed Paris with the arrows of Heracles. Paris might have been spared if his former mistress, the nymph Oenone, had agreed to heal him, but she refused and then hanged herself.

The death of Paris and possession of Heracles' weapons did not change the stalemate, so Calchas told the Greeks that only Helenus, the Trojan seer and prince, knew how Troy's downfall might be brought about. Odysseus captured Helenus on Mount Ida. Helenus bore a personal grudge against Troy, having fought for Helen after Paris died and having lost her, and he was willing to betray the city. First, the Greeks had to bring Pelops' bones back to Asia from Greece. Agamemnon accomplished this. Second, they had to bring Achilles' son Neoptolemus into the war, and a group of Greeks went to Scyros to get him. Third, the Greeks had to steal the Palladium, a sacred image of Athena, from the goddess's temple in Troy. Diomedes and Odysseus undertook the dangerous mission. Once in Troy Odysseus was recognized by Helen, who saw through his disguise but did not give him away. The two heroes seized the sacred image of Athena and escaped unharmed.

If Odysseus claimed credit for the notion of the huge wooden horse, Athena had given the idea to another. Nevertheless, Odysseus helped the plan succeed. A great horse of wood was constructed under Greek supervision, one with a hollow belly to hold several soldiers. One night this horse was brought to the Trojan plain and warriors climbed in under Odysseus' direction. The rest of the Greeks burned their camps and sailed off to wait behind the nearby island of Tenedos.

The next morning the Trojans found the Greeks gone and the huge, mysterious horse sitting before Troy. They also discovered a Greek named Sinon, whom they took captive. Odysseus had primed Sinon with plausible stories about the Greek departure, the wooden horse, and his own presence there. Sinon told Priam and the others that Athena had deserted the Greeks because of the theft of the Palladium. Without her help they were lost and had best depart. But to get home safely they had to have a human sacrifice, and Sinon was chosen, yet he got away and hid. The horse had been left to placate the angry goddess, and the Greeks were hoping the Trojans would desecrate it, earning Athena's hatred. These lies convinced Priam and many Trojans. However, Cassandra and a priest named Laocoön warned that the horse was full of soldiers. No one believed Cassandra anyhow. And when Laocoön hurled a spear at the horse a hostile god sent two large snakes to strangle him and his sons. The Trojans needed no further proof: they drew the gigantic horse inside their city gates to honor Athena.

That night the soldiers crept from the horse, killed the sentries, and opened the gates to let the Greek army in. The Greeks set fires throughout the city, began massacring the inhabitants, and looted. The Trojan resistance was ineffectual. King Priam was killed by Neoptolemus. And by morning all but a few Trojans were dead. Of Trojan males only Aeneas, with his father and son, had escaped the slaughter. Hector's young son Astyanax was thrown from the walls of the city. The women who were left went into concubinage as spoils of war. And the princess Polyxena, whom Achilles had loved, was sacrificed brutally upon the tomb of the dead hero. Troy was devastated. Hera and Athena had their revenge upon Paris and his city.

Commentary

The legend of the Trojan War comes from a number of sources besides Homer. *The Iliad* deals with the central part of the tale, from the quarrel between Agamemnon and Achilles to Hector's funeral. This is the heart of the story, but the legend as a whole has a unity of its own. Schliemann's excavations at Troy and subsequent investigations make it somewhat likely that a siege may have taken place in the Mycenaean period. But regardless of actual historical fact and despite discrepancies in various treatments of the legend this story has a reality and a coherence that seem remarkable.

The unity lies in the interweaving of the divine and the human. On a purely human level the tale makes sense. Thus, Paris, a lecherous prince, abducts Helen. The Greeks are bound by honor to seek revenge on both Paris and the city that harbors him. The war lasts ten years, and the same honor that brought the Greeks occasions internecine fights of great bitterness. Both sides fight valiantly, but fighting fails to bring Troy low. The Greeks turn to oracles, which produce nothing. Finally, they turn to their own wits and work out a strategem that wins the war.

On the divine level the story makes equal sense. Hera and Athena hate Paris for preferring Aphrodite, and they hate the city that bred him. Being goddesses of power and bravery, they aid the Greeks in every possible way, even in giving them the plan that brings Troy down. But everything that happened was known beforehand. The war was fated before Paris was born. Some principle of Necessity wrote the whole scenario.

The human and the divine interact through dreams, oracles, and inspiration in battle. And often the gods themselves put in a personal appearance to aid their favorites. Dreams and oracles reveal the will of the gods, but inspired fighting shows the gods' favor. Of course that favor is rather precarious, yet by means of it a hero wins the only thing in life worth winning—fame, glory in posterity. The Greeks looked back wistfully to the period of the Trojan War and earlier as an age of true greatness.

One might think that a race which values courage in battle to the degree the Greeks did would be blind to the squalor of war. But this legend shows nothing of the kind. Ruthless slaughter, meanness and trickery, the degradation of death —these are set forth without mitigation in a realistic light. Hector and Achilles are basically tragic figures, for they know the terrible doom that must fall on them, but they act out their destinies in battle with valor.

An outstanding incident in this tale comes as Hector faces Achilles. Achilles has nothing to lose, while Hector bears the weight of Troy on his shoulders. Seeing that Achilles is full of divine power, Hector weakens and runs even though he is a man of great courage. Athena has to trick him into making a stand, and Achilles slays him. Dying, Hector begs his killer to allow his parents to ransom his body, and the last thing he hears is Achilles' gloating refusal. But Achilles has set his own doom in motion. This episode prefigures the fall of Troy in a heart-rending way. The foremost hero of Troy has been slain by the foremost hero of Greece, who must shortly die in turn. Human choice and divine inevitability are interwoven here in tragic terms. But the entire legend of the Trojan War bears that same tragic stamp.

THE RETURNS

Having accomplished their aim in sacking Troy, the Greeks now had to face the problem of getting back to their various kingdoms. This was a problem, for the gods had scores to settle with many Greeks. Soon after the Greeks set sail a fierce storm arose that blew much of the Greek fleet far off course.

Of those who went by ship Agamemnon was one of the few that escaped the storm and reached home easily. But immediately upon his return Agamemnon's wife, Clytemnestra, and her lover, Aegisthus, slew him and his followers, including Cassandra, at the banquet table. Clytemnestra had never forgiven her husband for sacrificing Iphigenia.

Menelaus had resolved to kill Helen when he found her in Troy, but on seeing her naked breasts he lost his determination and took her again as his wife. After offending Athena, Menelaus and Helen were caught in the storm, lost most of their ships, and were blown to Crete and Egypt. Unable to return to Sparta because of adverse winds, Menelaus began trading. Eight years later he wrested the secret of getting home from the prophetic sea god Proteus, master of changes. And having propitiated Athena, Menelaus was able to sail to Sparta with Helen, returning a rich man. When the two of them died they went to the Isles of the Blessed, being favored relations of Zeus.

The lesser Ajax, who had raped Cassandra in the temple of Athena while plundering Troy, was shipwrecked on his way home. Scrambling onto the rocks, he rejoiced at having escaped the vengeance of the gods. But Poseidon split the rock to which he clung and drowned him. Athena then exacted an annual tribute of two maidens from Ajax's fellow Locrians to be sent to Troy.

Bitterly resentful of the Greeks, Nauplius caused many of their ships to smash on the Euboean coast by lighting a deceptive beacon. Philoctetes, who still nursed a grudge against the Greeks for their shabby treatment of him, did not return to Greece but sailed to Italy, where he founded two cities.

The prophet Calchas made it to Colophon, where he met the seer Mopsus. He engaged Mopsus in a contest of prophecy, which he lost. Calchas then died.

Achilles' son Neoptolemus had established himself as a valiant fighter at Troy. Warned against ruling his home kingdom, he went instead to Epirus and became the Molossian king. Neoptolemus went to Delphi to demand retribution from Apollo, who had helped kill his father. When the priestess refused he robbed and burned the temple. Later he returned to Delphi, where he was killed in a dispute over sacrificial meat. The devotees of Apollo then erected a new temple over his grave.

Of all the Greeks only the wise Nestor sailed swiftly home and enjoyed the fruits of old age in peace, surrounded by stalwart sons. His virtues of prudence and piety had enabled him to live to see three generations of heroes.

ODYSSEUS' ADVENTURES

Of the Greeks who made it back to their homes Odysseus was fated to wander the longest—a full ten years—and he knew it. Among the Trojan women Hecuba fell to him, an old harridan now who could not forgive the way Odysseus had thrown her grandson Astyanax from the walls of Troy. Odysseus' ships were hit by the storm raised by Athena and were blown to Thrace. Sick of Hecuba's insults, he and his men stoned her to death.

In Thrace Odysseus sacked the city of the Cicones, sparing only a priest of Apollo, who rewarded him with a skin of potent wine. The Cicones that neighbored the city then attacked, killing many of Odysseus' men and driving the rest back to their ships. Storms blew the ships to Libya and the land of the Lotus-eaters, where an exploring party accepted the Lotus fruit from the natives and lost all memories of home. Odysseus had to recover these sailors forcibly.

Setting sail again they came to the island of the Cyclopes, a huge race of monsters with one eye in the middle of their foreheads. Unwittingly Odysseus and a scouting party feasted in the cave of Polyphemus, a son of Poseidon. The Cyclops returned, shut the Greeks in with a huge boulder, and ate two men apiece at each meal. Finally Odysseus devised a plan of escape. He and his remaining men blinded the giant in a drunken sleep with a sharpened pole. Then as Polyphemus was letting his sheep out of the cave to pasture, counting each one by touch, Odysseus and his men got out by clinging to the underbellies of the sheep. Returning to their ship, Odysseus jeered at Polyphemus, telling him that he, Odysseus, had blinded him. In a rage the giant hurled two great boulders at the ship that nearly swamped it. Then Polyphemus prayed to his father Poseidon to cause Odysseus as much trouble as possible.

Odysseus and his men then came to the island of Aeolus, the keeper of the winds. Aeolus entertained them for a month and presented Odysseus with a skin containing all the winds but the west wind, which would blow him home. Odysseus arrived within sight of his home, Ithaca, but he fell asleep from exhaustion. His men opened the sack of winds, thinking it held wine, and all the ships were blown back to Aeolus, who refused them further help.

Next Odysseus and his ships arrived at the land of the Laestrygonians, a savage race of cannibals. All but Odysseus put their vessels into the harbor lined with cliffs. The scouting party was attacked by the Laestrygonians, who bombarded the ships with boulders and sank them. Only Odysseus and his crew survived. The rest of the Greeks were eaten.

With but one ship left Odysseus sailed east and arrived at the Island of Dawn, which was inhabited by Circe, the sorceress. The group of men sent to explore the place were feasted by Circe and then were turned into swine. Learning of this, Odysseus went after Circe, and on his way the god Hermes gave him the herb *moly* to resist her enchantment. Circe invited him to eat, but her spell was ineffective, and Odysseus compelled her to restore the swine to human shape. He remained with her long enough to father three sons on her. Homesick, Odysseus was advised by Circe to journey to the world's end, enter Hades, and consult the seer Teiresias about his future and how he might appease Poseidon. In Hades, Teiresias told Odysseus of the difficulties he faced and of what he must do to placate Poseidon. Odysseus saw many dead notables there, including many of his companions at Troy. With his new knowledge he returned to Circe, who showed him how to get safely past the Sirens.

When Odysseus neared the island of the Sirens he had his men fill their ears with wax, for the singing of the Sirens lured sailors to their deaths on the rocks. He had himself tied to the mast so that he might hear their singing and still survive. Once that danger was over, the ship had to pass between two cliffs in a strait that had the whirlpool of Charybdis. In trying to avoid the maelstrom Odysseus came too close to the cliff of the monster Scylla, who seized six of Odysseus' sailors. The next stop was the island of the sun god Helios, which nourished the god's sacred cattle. When Odysseus fell asleep his men, who were starving, slaughtered a number of the cattle. For this impiety Zeus struck Odysseus' ship with a thunderbolt, and only Odysseus escaped alive. Clinging to a piece of the ship, Odysseus was borne toward the whirlpool of Charybdis, but he grabbed a tree branch hanging over the water, waited till the timbers re-emerged, and floated off to nearby Ogygia.

Ogygia was inhabited by the nymph Calypso, who welcomed Odysseus and made him her lover. He remained with her seven years and grew increasingly homesick, sitting on the beach each day in a desolate mood. While Poseidon was off visiting the Ethiopians, Zeus arranged for Odysseus to depart, sending Hermes to bid Calypso release him. Calypso gave Odysseus an axe with which he fashioned a raft.

Poseidon returned from his Ethiopian junket to find Odysseus sailing along on a raft. The god washed him overboard and almost drowned him, but Odysseus was spared by the goddess Ino, who gave him her magic veil to tie around his waist. And after two days of swimming Odysseus found a beach on which to sleep. He was awakened by maidens who were playing ball after doing the washing. Odysseus gently addressed Nausicaä, the daughter of King Alcinoüs. She led him to her father. At first the Phaeacians, who lived on the island, were cool to Odysseus, but he bested them in a stone-throwing contest and they accepted him. King Alcinoüs listened to the story of Odysseus' wanderings, presented him with rich gifts, and furnished him a ship to get to Ithaca, his home. The Phaeacian sailors, seeing that Odysseus was sleeping, left him on the Ithacan shore and departed. But Poseidon resented the way they had helped Odysseus and changed the ship and crew to stone.

In the twenty years that Odysseus had been absent his wife Penelope had been besieged with suitors who had moved into the palace and proceeded to devour Odysseus' wealth. Penelope had promised to choose one of them as king when she finished a tapestry on which she was working, but what she did by day she would unravel at night. Things on the island had become risky for Odysseus' teenage son Telemachus, so Athena had guided him to Nestor's court and then to Sparta and the court of Menelaus, where he sought word of his father. Menelaus received the young man royally and assured Telemachus that his father was alive. Telemachus then returned home, where Athena gave him the idea of visiting the hut of the swineherd Eumaeus. There he found an old beggar who suddenly revealed himself to be Odysseus. Father and son embraced and wept. Then they made plans for ridding the palace of the arrogant suitors.

Still disguised as a beggar, Odysseus went to the palace. An old dog of his—named Argos—recognized him and died. The leader of the suitors, Antinoüs, struck the beggar. Then Penelope came to receive bridal gifts from the suitors and requested that the beggar come to her room. Odysseus kept his disguise, telling Penelope a pack of lies about his adventures. But while bathing him his old nurse, Eurycleia, recognized him by a hunting scar he had acquired years before, so he made her keep silent. Odysseus had Telemachus remove the weapons from the great banquet hall. The next day Penelope announced that she would marry the man who could string Odysseus' great bow and shoot an arrow through twelve rings in a line. After all the suitors had tried and failed the beggar asked to try. The suitors protested, but Telemachus stood up for the beggar, who then strung the bow and fired the arrow through the rings.

Giving a shout of triumph the beggar showed himself to be Odysseus and fired arrow after arrow into the host of suitors. The suitors sought their weapons and began to put up some resistance, but when Odysseus ran out of arrows Telemachus brought him armor, spears, and swords. The father and son, who had stationed themselves in the doorway, cut the suitors down as they tried to escape. And at last the suitors were all dead. Only a poet and a priest were left. Odysseus killed the priest and spared the poet. Then he made the palace maids who had slept with the suitors clean up the mess, and after that he hanged them. Having set his house in order, Odysseus then revealed himself to Penelope, who had kept to her chamber. The two were happily reunited.

Odysseus' wanderings, however, were not at an end. He had to battle the relatives of the suitors. Athena proposed a truce and submitted the dispute to the king of the Epirot Islands, who decided that Odysseus should go into exile from Ithaca for ten years, that Telemachus should rule in his stead, and that the relatives should repay the losses that the suitors had caused. Odysseus undertook to placate Poseidon as Teiresias had advised. He marched inland on Epirus to a place where the natives had never seen an oar and mistook the one he carried for a winnowing-bat. There he sacrificed to Poseidon, who forgave him for blinding Polyphemus.

When ten years were up he returned to Ithaca, where he died at sea in a fight with his own son by Circe, Telegonus.

Commentary

Most of the legends here have their source in Homer's *Odyssey*. An interesting thing about these stories is that two of the gods who were of the greatest assistance to the Greeks at Troy, Athena and Poseidon, proved their greatest enemies as they returned to their homes. The gods, of course, were just as concerned with their personal honor as the heroes themselves, and to offend their pride or harm their favorites was to court disaster.

Nevertheless, a hero like Odysseus proves his mettle when faced with the opposition of the gods. Odysseus is shrewd, tough, clear-sighted, experienced, a man very well equipped to brave adversity. Like a few other heroes he is intensely self-reliant, confident of his own powers against the buffetings of fate.

Odysseus lives about sixty years roughly, and of these he spends thirty abroad—the years of his maturity. He leaves Ithaca as a hardy young man to take part in the Trojan War, which lasts ten years. Moreover, he goes very reluctantly. After another ten years of wandering, which had been ordained by the gods, he returns home, now a man in his forties. But then he is exiled shortly thereafter for a further ten years and comes back a man verging on old age. To be sure, Odysseus thrives on adventure, for that is how a man tests his prowess. But when he has time to reflect, as he does on Calypso's island, he is lacerated by homesickness. The gods could scarcely find a better way to punish a man whose heart is attached to home.

The Greeks felt a special affection for Odysseus because he reflected a number of Greek qualities. A wanderer living by his wits, taking part in a great national war, traveling far and wide, meeting emergencies with a cool head, and longing for his native home, Odysseus is a recognizable Greek type. But beyond that he is the survivor, the man who comes through at all hazards by his brains, his brawn, and his fortitude, plus an ounce of luck. Odysseus embodies the stubborn will of the ancient Greeks to overcome fate and create a culture that centered on man. The Romans, who called him Ulysses, disliked him for his treachery and cunning. He had these traits too, but they are far less important than those which enabled him to endure with his human dignity intact.

BRIEF SUMMARIES OF OTHER MYTHS

AEACUS

Zeus lay with Aegina on the island of Oenopia, and she gave birth to Aeacus, who became king and named the island after her. Hera had never forgiven Aegina for tempting Zeus, so she visited the island with plague and famine, which killed all but Aeacus and his family. Aeacus then prayed to Zeus, who created a new race of men out of ants—the Myrmidons, renowned for their tenacity, thrift, and patience. Aeacus himself became famous for his integrity and piety. When he died Zeus made him one of the three judges of the underworld, along with Minos and Rhadamanthus.

ALCYONE AND CEYX

Ceyx, the son of the morning star, married Alcyone, the daughter of Aeolus. They were devoted to each other, and in their bliss Alcyone began calling herself Hera and her husband Zeus. For this presumption Zeus destroyed Ceyx as he sailed to consult an oracle. Alcyone, who had been left at home, then learned of Ceyx's death in a dream, so she plunged herself into the sea. But a god took pity on the pair, changing them into kingfishers. The female kingfisher lays her eggs and hatches them in a sea-nest during the two weeks in winter when the sea is calm. This time is called the Halcyon Days.

ARISTAEUS

Apollo noticed a beautiful girl named Cyrene as she fought off a lion while tending her father's sheep in Thessaly. He fell in love with her and asked the Centaur Chiron's advice about abducting her. Chiron said she would become a great queen in Libya, so Apollo carried her off to that land, where she gave birth to Aristaeus. Aristaeus, "the best," became proficient in agriculture: tending olive trees, making cheese, raising cattle, and cultivating bee hives. However, he made the mistake of lusting after Orpheus' bride, Eurydice, who died as he pursued her. His bees started dying, so his mother Cyrene advised him to capture the sea god Proteus. Finding Proteus, Aristaeus compelled him to prophesy. The god told him to make sacrifices to the Dryads and to Orpheus. Upon doing so the bees revived, and the art of beekeeping was preserved for posterity.

ASCLEPIUS

Apollo loved the beautiful Coronis, who proved unfaithful to him. The angry god killed her but saved her unborn infant, his own son Asclepius, whom he placed in the care of the wise Centaur Chiron. Asclepius learned the art of medicine, in which he had a miraculous skill. However, when he brought a dead man back to life he overstepped himself, offending Hades. Zeus killed the physician with a thunderbolt. But even after his death he continued to cure the sick in temples of healing by appearing in dreams and giving remedies.

CASTOR AND POLYDEUCES

These twin sons of Leda, Castor and Polydeuces, had different fathers. Castor, who became famous as a horse tamer and soldier, was sired by King Tyndareus of Sparta, while Polydeuces, who became an invincible boxer, was fathered by Zeus. These Spartan heroes were inseparable, undertaking many heroic missions together. They went on the Calydonian boar hunt; they shipped with Jason on the *Argo;* they rescued their sister Helen from Theseus. On their last expedition Castor was killed by a cattle breeder named Idas in a fight over some oxen. Polydeuces took revenge and then prayed to Zeus that he might die and share his own immortality with Castor. Zeus granted the request. The brothers were to spend one day in Hades, the next on Olympus, and so on. They were venerated as the protectors of sailors.

THE DANAÏDS

King Danaüs of Egypt had fifty daughters. His brother Aegyptus had fifty sons who wanted to marry their cousins, but the girls and their father were utterly opposed to it. They fled to Argos and took sanctuary, but despite the aid of the people of Argos the sons of Aegyptus prevailed. Danaüs presided over the wedding rites but secretly gave each of his daughters a dagger. That night the Danaïds slew the bridegrooms. Only one did not: Hypermnestra refused to stab Lynceus, for which her father threw her in prison. Hypermnestra's sisters, however, had a worse fate and were sentenced to carry water in leaky jars for all eternity in Hades.

ENDYMION

In Caria there is a Mount Latmus, which has a cave containing the shepherd Endymion, a youth of surpassing beauty. Selene, the moon, found him there one night, lay beside him, and kissed his eyes. He sleeps there permanently in a magic trance, never growing older, as a captive of the moon.

MELAMPUS

A famed seer and physician, Melampus acquired his prophetic powers in a strange way. When his servants killed a pair of snakes Melampus buried them and raised their young. As he was sleeping two of his snakes crawled up and licked his ears, which gave him the ability to understand the speech of all living creatures. His brother Bion wanted to marry Pero, but her father demanded the cattle of Iphiclus in return for his daughter. Melampus offered his aid, but was caught and jailed in trying to steal the cattle. In prison he heard the termites saying the building would collapse soon. He told this to Iphiclus' father, and it came true. Iphiclus' father then said Melampus could have the cattle if he found the reason for Iphiclus being childless. Melampus learned the secret from a vulture, obtained the cattle, and saw his brother happily married to Pero.

MIDAS

Dionysus passed through Phrygia on his way to India, and there his drunken follower Silenus wandered into the rose gardens of King Midas, the wealthiest man in the world. Midas entertained Silenus for several days and learned the Mysteries of Dionysus from him. Then Midas led the reveler back to Dionysus, who promised to grant anything he wished for. The king wished that all he touched would turn to gold, and Dionysus granted the wish. When Midas tried to eat, his food turned to gold, so the starving man returned to Dionysus to get him to retract his gift. The god told Midas to wash in the River Pactolus, which he did, thereby turning the sands to gold but curing himself. On another occasion Midas preferred Pan to Apollo in a musical contest, so Apollo gave him a pair of asses' ears. Midas hid his ears under a cap, and only his barber knew of them, but he had promised to tell no one. Burdened with this secret the barber went down to the shore, scooped out a hole and whispered, "Midas has asses' ears," into it. The next year reeds grew in that spot, and as the wind rustled through them the reeds repeated the secret to everyone who came past.

NARCISSUS

Narcissus was a youth possessed of incredible beauty, and while everyone who saw him loved him, males as well as females, he spurned them all through pride. The hapless nymph Echo, whom Hera had punished by turning her speech into a repetition of what others said, came across Narcissus in a glade and pleaded with him, using his own words, to love her. He rejected her. Artemis grew angry and caused him to fall in love with himself. Narcissus came to a clear pond and became enraptured when he saw his reflection. He sat down and gazed longingly at himself hour upon hour. At length he desperately killed himself with a knife, unable to bear his self-love, and where his blood fell grew up the narcissus flower, which has medicinal properties. Echo repeated his dying word, "Alas!"

ORION

Orion, the huge, handsome son of Poseidon, was a hunter of Boeotia. Courting Merope, he grew impatient of her father's conditions and raped her, whereupon her father blinded him and threw him out. Advised by an oracle, Orion traveled east to the point where Helios arose from Ocean. Dawn fell in love with Orion and slept with him. Helios, the sun, cured his sight. Then the hunter went searching for Merope's father to get revenge. But Artemis dissuaded him and he became her hunting companion. Fearing for the chastity of his sister Artemis, Apollo sent a large scorpion to chase Orion. Unable to subdue the vicious beast, Orion set out across the water. Apollo persuaded Artemis to shoot the bobbing object out on the waves and she pierced Orion's head. She then set his image up among the stars, where it was pursued by the constellation of the scorpion.

OTUS AND EPHIALTES

The gigantic sons of Poseidon, Otus and Ephialtes knew they could not be killed by gods or other men, and in their self-confidence they laid siege to Olympus. Ephialtes intended to rape Hera, and Otus swore he'd rape Artemis. They captured Ares and locked him in a brass jar for thirteen months. Artemis then offered to lay with Otus on the island of Naxos, which made Ephialtes jealous. On Naxos a quarrel arose between the two giants. Changing herself into a white doe, Artemis sprang between them. They seized their spears and attempted to slay the doe, but they killed each other instead, putting an end to their war against the gods.

PHAËTHON

The sun, Helios, had a son named Phaëthon who yearned to drive his father's fiery chariot across the sky. Helios made the mistake of promising the boy anything he wanted and could not go back on his word. Despite Helios' warnings Phaëthon insisted. The boy began to climb through the sky easily enough, but the horses soon knew they had an inexperienced driver and began racing wildly, careening against the stars and then swooping toward the earth, setting the world in flames. To save the earth Zeus struck the terrified boy with a thunderbolt, killing him instantly. The horses rushed into the sea.

SISYPHUS

Renowned for his cleverness and knavery, Sisyphus lived by thieving. When the famous thief Autolycus began stealing his cattle Sisyphus marked the hooves and caught him, and then seduced his daughter. He treacherously ousted his brother from the Thessalian throne. But he overreached himself in telling the river god Asopus where Zeus had abducted his daughter Aegina. Asopus nearly avenged himself on Zeus, so Zeus ordered his brother Hades to fetch Sisyphus to the underworld. But Sisyphus tricked Hades into putting on his own handcuffs and kept him captive until Ares released the god of death. Sisyphus had told his wife not to bury him, and when he went to Hell he complained of this dishonor and was allowed to return to the land of the living to avenge himself. But he refused to return, and finally Hermes had to drag him back. In the underworld for good, Sisyphus was sentenced to roll a huge boulder up a hill, one which kept rolling back down after reaching the top. This was his eternal punishment.

TITHONUS

Eos, the dawn, had slept with Ares, the lover of Aphrodite. So Aphrodite revenged herself by giving Eos an insatiable desire for young men. She took the Trojan prince Tithonus, among others, as her lover, and she asked Zeus to grant him immortality. Zeus did, but Eos had forgotten to request eternal youth as well, so Tithonus was fated to live forever and grow increasingly older. In time he withered into a parody of a man. His voice became shrill. And Eos shut the loathsome creature away in a closet, where it turned into a grasshopper.

Commentary

In this assorted collection of myths we see the spectrum of Greek mythological styles. There are the explanatory tales. "Aeacus" shows how the Myrmidons came about and accounts for their character. "Orion" relates how two constellations came to be. There are the heroic legends of "Castor and Polydeuces," "Otus and Ephialtes," and "Asclepius." There are cautionary legends such as "Phaëthon," "Narcissus," and "Alcyone and Ceyx." There are the folk tales of "Midas" and "Sisyphus." And there are such romanticized tales as "Endymion" and "Narcissus." If they lack the seriousness of the major Greek myths and legends, they still have value as entertaining stories.

Roman Mythology

INTRODUCTION

In contrast to that of the Greeks, Roman mythology seems arid and impoverished. As a rule the Romans were not myth-makers, and the myths they had were usually imported. The Roman gods were utilitarian, like the practical and unimaginative Romans themselves. These gods were expected to serve and protect men, and when they failed to be useful their worship was curtailed. This does not mean the Romans lacked religious sentiment. They had a pantheistic sense of the divinities present in nature. But their deepest religious feelings centered on the family and the state. When the Romans adopted the Greek gods from the third century B.C. on, these deities were simplified to conform to the Roman religion. Mars was the chief god of the imperial age, more honored than Jupiter, since he aided and symbolized the Roman conquests.

The writers who handled mythological subjects typically dealt with patriotic legends that glorified the Roman past, or in love tales. Thus they paid tribute to the state or to love, the basis of the family, in terms derived from Greek mythology. Sometimes in their borrowings they achieved true originality, as Vergil did in his epic poem, *The Aeneid,* or as Ovid did in his poetic compilation, *The Metamorphoses.* First we will examine the patriotic legends of Vergil and Livy to see what kept Roman civilization going, and then we will study the mythological love stories of Ovid, Apuleius, and Musaeus to learn some Roman conceptions of love.

THE ROMAN GODS

The gods listed immediately following were the Roman adaptations of the Greek gods. These had importance in both

Roman mythological writing and in the Roman religion. Then we will list some of the purely native gods, who were significant mainly for the Roman religion.

Jupiter, Jove (Zeus) reigned in the Roman pantheon and defended the state, a god of celestial phenomena and justice.

Juno (Hera), the wife of Jupiter, a goddess of motherhood and childbearing.

Saturn (Cronus), the father of Jupiter, ruled Italy during the Golden Age. The Saturnalia was held in his honor, a winter festival in which masters and slaves exchanged roles, a time of gift giving and license.

Mars (Ares), the son of Juno, was a highly respected god of war but also an agricultural deity. Thus he represented two primary Roman preoccupations—farming and fighting.

Vesta (Hestia) was a lovely goddess of the hearth and of sacrificial fire. Her temple was tended by the Vestal Virgins.

Ceres (Demeter) was a goddess of grain.

Minerva (Athena) was a warrior goddess who also presided over commerce.

Neptune (Poseidon) was lord of the sea.

Dis, Pluto (Hades) ruled the underworld of death.

Mercury (Hermes) was a god of commerce and messages.

Venus (Aphrodite), originally an agricultural goddess, was the deity of love, particularly sexual love.

Cupid (Eros), her son, was the god of erotic attraction.

Vulcan, Mulciber (Hephaestus) was a god of fire and warmth, of the forge and of volcanic eruptions.

Liber, Bacchus (Dionysus) was the god of wine and drunkenness.

Diana (Artemis) was a huntress, goddess of the woods and moon.

Apollo was the god of truth and light, as in Greece.

Proserpina (Persephone), a goddess of spring, the daughter of Ceres and wife of Pluto.

The ***Numina*** were vague, protective powers that inhabited nature and presided over daily human activities, the earliest gods.

Janus was the god of beginnings, of doorways and public gates, of departures and returns. The statue of Janus in his temple had two faces, a young one that looked toward the rising sun and an old one that faced the setting sun. At his temple in Rome the doors were shut only in times of peace, which were extremely rare.

The ***Lares*** and ***Penates*** were mainly gods of the family. A ***Lar*** was a protective ancestral spirit, while the ***Penates*** were household gods, guardians of the hearth and storerooms. Each Roman family had its own special gods. However, Roman cities had public Lares and Penates to safeguard them.

Priapus, an ugly god with huge genitals, promoted fertility.

Sylvanus and ***Faunus*** were rustic gods of the forest and possessed goat-shanks, like Pan. ***Fauns*** were woodland goat-men, and have often been confused with Satyrs, who had horses' haunches.

Flora was a goddess of flowers, fruits, and springtime.

The ***Manes*** were benevolent spirits of the dead, good souls, as opposed to the ***Lemurs*** (also ***Larvae***), which were evil discarnates.

PATRIOTIC LEGENDS

AENEAS

When the Greeks entered Troy to devastate it the ghost of Hector told Aeneas to leave. Aided by his mother Venus, Aeneas fought the Greeks and made his way out of the doomed city with his father Anchises and his son Iulus. He joined a group of Trojan comrades and together they built some ships with which they sailed to Thrace, where Aeneas hoped to set up a colony. Warned off by a Trojan ghost who had been murdered by the Thracians, they made for Delos, where an oracle of Apollo told the Trojans to return to the land of their ancestors. Thinking that Apollo meant Crete, they moved to this island, which was uninhabited, only to be dogged by pestilence. At length Aeneas dreamed that his future home lay far to the west in Italy, from which the Trojan Dardanus had come long before. Aeneas now knew where his destiny was taking him.

Having left Crete, the Trojans were caught in a storm that drove them up the western coast of Greece. Driven off by those birdlike monsters, the Harpies, they sailed to Epirus and found Prince Helenus of Troy married to Hector's wife, Andromache. When Troy fell Andromache had been taken captive by Achilles' son Pyrrhus (Neoptolemus in Greek), and when he was killed she married Helenus. The pair entertained Aeneas and his comrades. Helenus foretold that they would have a perilous time getting to Italy, and he warned them against the Strait of Messina, where Scylla and Charybdis waited. Further, they were to sail to Cumae sometime in the future, where Aeneas would consult the Sibyl, a prophetess.

Next the Trojans stopped briefly on the eastern coast of Italy to worship in their new homeland, but the place was inhabited by Greeks and dangerous. Sailing south, Aeneas and his men narrowly escaped Scylla and the whirlpool of Charybdis. They landed on Sicily near Mount Aetna to find a ragged sailor who had been abandoned by Ulysses (Odysseus). The fellow told them of Cyclopes nearby, and no sooner had they put out to sea than Polyphemus charged into the water after them. At Drepanum on Sicily's western coast they were well received by King Acestes, a man of Trojan origin, and there Aeneas' father Anchises died.

The goddess Juno hated all Trojans because of Paris, but she especially disliked Aeneas and his men, knowing that in the ages to come their descendants would destroy her favorite city of Carthage, which was now being built. She bribed Aeolus to unleash a dire storm on Aeneas and his ships. The typhoon scattered the fleet and sank one ship. Finally Neptune calmed the sea, and Aeneas put into harbor with seven ships on the African coast. The Trojans warmed themselves over fires while Aeneas killed deer for food.

Meanwhile Venus complained to Jupiter of her son Aeneas' many misfortunes, but Jupiter reassured her that Aeneas, after many trials, would found a great nation. This was his destiny, and even Juno would become reconciled to it.

As Aeneas and his comrade Achates scouted this new land they came upon Venus disguised as a huntress, and she told them they were in Libya near Carthage, a city ruled by the beautiful queen Dido. Dido had fled from Tyre with some loyal followers, and here in Libya they were building a new city called Carthage.

Venus departed but left Aeneas and Achates concealed in a mist so that they might enter the city unseen. The pair came to a temple of Juno, which was adorned with murals of the Trojan War. Inside they found Dido performing her queenly duties. They also discovered their own companions who had been lost at sea asking Dido's permission to remain and repair their battered ships, which she granted. They were even welcome to stay in Carthage.

Then Aeneas stepped forward, greeted his lost comrades and requested Dido's hospitality and aid. Dido was full of admiration and pity for the handsome commander, but Venus sent Cupid to turn her admiration into love, thereby insuring Aeneas' safety. As Aeneas recounted the fall of Troy and his own adventures Dido grew enamored of him. The lovesick queen yearned for him, and Juno decided to marry the two with the consent of Venus. As Aeneas and Dido were hunting a storm came upon them, and seeking shelter in a cave they made love. Rumor spread quickly of the affair, and Dido's former suitor Iarbus, king of Libya, was enraged. Then Jupiter sent Mercury to remind Aeneas of his promised homeland in Italy, and the hero reluctantly made plans to depart in secret. But Dido learned of it and pleaded with him to stay. Her words were useless; the will of the gods must be obeyed. As Aeneas and his ships were ready to sail, Dido called upon her descendants to avenge his treachery. She committed suicide upon her own funeral pyre. Out at sea Aeneas saw the flames of her pyre and was filled with remorse.

The Trojans reached Drepanum again, where they celebrated funeral games for Anchises. There Juno caused the Trojan women to burn four of their boats. Leaving the sick and weary to settle at Drepanum, Aeneas took his hardiest Trojans to Italy. To make sure of their safety Venus and Neptune ordained that one man must die—the pilot Palinurus, who slept at the helm, fell into the sea, and was drowned.

On reaching Cumae, a town in western Italy, Aeneas went to the temple of Apollo, which had been designed by Daedalus. There he found the Sibyl, who prophesied that he must wage war to gain a bride and establish a city. Aeneas persuaded the Sibyl to direct him through the underworld, where he wanted to see his father Anchises. He must obtain the Golden Bough of

Proserpina to enter. Then the Sibyl led him into the earth beside Lake Avernus. Descending into the realm of the dead, they saw specters, Charon the ferryman, all sorts of departed spirits, including the pouting Dido. They finally came to the Elysian Fields, which was reserved for the blessed dead. There they met Anchises, who described the operations of the cosmos, the way men are purified to enter Elysium, and the long line of Aeneas' descendants who would rule Rome and make it great, right down to Augustus Caesar. Then Aeneas and his guide made their way back to the world of the living, where Aeneas joined his comrades. They sailed north along the coast and up the Tiber River.

At last Aeneas has arrived at his destined home. The place was Latium, ruled by a King Latinus who had a beautiful daughter named Lavinia. It was foretold that Lavinia would marry a foreigner. When Aeneas arrived Latinus gave him a warm welcome, but Queen Amata wanted Lavinia to marry the Rutulian, Turnus. Turnus became furiously jealous of Aeneas, for he loved Lavinia and wished to marry her. The people of Latium resented these upstart Trojans. So when Juno caused Iulus, the son of Aeneas, to kill a pet deer, war broke out between the Trojans and all the neighboring peoples, who assembled under Turnus, a strong and fearless warrior. The Volscians joined the massing forces and were led by Camilla, the beautiful virgin warrior.

Knowing that a huge army was gathering against him and his men, Aeneas ordered a camp built. One night the river god Tiber appeared to him, telling him to travel upriver to Pallanteum and seek aid. In Pallanteum Aeneas was given two hundred men by Evander, who disliked Latinus and his people. Evander's own son Pallas also joined Aeneas. And Evander advised the hero to get further help from the Etruscans of the north, who hated Mezentius, their renegade king who had sided with Turnus. Venus brought Aeneas armor made by Vulcan. On the shield were several scenes depicting the future history of Rome.

Turnus and his army attacked the Trojan camp while Aeneas was seeking the aid of the Etruscans. He burned the Trojan ships, which Neptune changed into sea nymphs at the bidding of Cybele. Aeneas had warned his men to stay inside the ramparts during his absence. However, two men crept out by night to tell Aeneas what had happened. As they made their way through the hostile, sleeping Rutulians they killed many, but they in turn were caught and slain. These bold youths were Euryalus and Nisus. The next day their heads were paraded before the Trojan camp.

Iulus slew the boy Numanus as he taunted the Trojans. Apollo then warned Iulus, who was a youth as well, to stay out of the fighting until he was older. That day the enemy burned a Trojan tower, and in the confusion the Trojans opened a gate. Before they could close it Turnus had made his way inside and began slaughtering men like sheep. But the Trojans regrouped under two able captains and forced Turnus to retreat to the Tiber, which he had to swim to reach safety.

Aeneas returned that night with a huge Etruscan army in thirty ships. The beleaguered Trojans rejoined. At dawn the ships made for the beach, and Aeneas leapt into the water to attack the foe. His furious slaughter made the Latins quail. Evander's son Pallas led his cavalry against Mezentius' son Lausus. But Turnus came to Lausus' aid and killed Pallas, roughly stripping the lad of his belt. When Aeneas heard of Pallas' death he charged with new fury into the Latin army and wounded Mezentius. Lausus sought to hold off Aeneas to allow his father to escape, and Aeneas tried to persuade the young man to retreat. Lausus refused and bravely died in combat with Aeneas, who respected the youth's corpse. Encountering Mezentius Aeneas killed him but took no pleasure in it, even though the man was evil.

A twelve-day truce was called in which both sides burned their dead on pyres and mourned. In Latium Queen Amata and Turnus prepared for further war. The Amazonian Camilla plotted with Turnus to ambush Aeneas and his troops as they rode through a narrow pass. In the fighting that followed, Camilla and her Volscians did great damage to the Etruscan army, but Camilla was slain and the disheartened Turnus called off the ambush.

Another truce followed in which King Latinus and Queen Amata tried to persuade Turnus to withdraw and allow Aeneas to wed Lavinia. Instead, Turnus challenged Aeneas to single combat before both armies. The next morning Aeneas and Iulus rode out to meet Turnus and Latinus. Before the assembled throng Aeneas promised that if he lost, his son would leave the territory forever, but if he won he would treat the Latins generously and build a city in honor of his bride Lavinia.

Juno sent Turnus' immortal sister, the numph Juturna, to spread confusion. Some Rutulian shot an arrow at Aeneas, hitting him. A general melee broke out as Aeneas withdrew, and Turnus waded into the dismayed Trojans, killing them freely. Venus quickly helped to heal her son's wound, so Aeneas returned to the fray, hunting for Turnus, who managed to elude him in a chariot drawn by Juturna. After hours of pursuit Aeneas decided to attack Latium. While the Trojans assaulted the city gates with battering rams, Queen Amata assumed that Turnus was dead and hanged herself. The Trojans felled a tower of the city, which prompted Turnus to quit fleeing and meet Aeneas head on. For a long time their duel was in doubt. Both men inflicted wounds and suffered them. But then Turnus' weapon shattered, so he turned to flee, and Aeneas chased him on limping legs. Juno saw the contest was already settled, but she exacted a promise from Jupiter that the Trojans and Latins would unite as a single people. Aeneas caught up with Turnus, crippling him. Turnus begged the Trojan to let him return to his father. Aeneas was on the verge of granting the request, but then he saw the belt Turnus had stripped from the dead Pallas. With a yell of victory Aeneas struck Turnus the death blow.

Needless to say, Aeneas married the Latin princess Lavinia and built the city of Lavinium. Through his Trojan son Iulus (also called Ascanius) he founded the line of Alban kings, which would result in the founding of Rome. By his strength, courage, piety, and steadfastness he exemplified the finest qualities his successors would possess.

ROMULUS AND REMUS

King Numitor of Alba Longa had an only child, Rhea Silvia. When Numitor was deposed and exiled by his younger brother Amulius the new king made Rhea Silvia a Vestal Virgin in order that she would not produce heirs to the throne. However, the god Mars ravished her and she gave birth to the twins Romulus and Remus. Amulius then imprisoned Rhea Silvia and gave orders that her infants be drowned. A she-wolf found the twins by the banks of the Tiber and suckled them. The king's herdsman discovered them, a man named Faustulus who took Romulus and Remus home and raised them. They grew into hardy, brave young men who robbed bandits and shared the spoils with the shepherds. During the festival of the Lupercal, Remus was captured by brigands and eventually delivered to Numitor for judgment. It was revealed that the two brothers were Numitor's grandsons. To avenge Numitor, Romulus and Remus then killed Amulius and reestablished Numitor as king of Alba Longa.

That city had a surplus of males who wished to emigrate, and Romulus and Remus decided to start a new settlement. The two brothers were jealous of each other, both being ambitious. In a dispute Romulus slew Remus and named the settlement after himself—Rome. He established a sanctuary for fugitives, gave the Romans laws, laid down the proper forms of worship, and created the hundred patricians. Yet the lack of women troubled him, so he invited the neighboring people to Rome to celebrate the Consualia in honor of Consus, a forerunner of Neptune. The Sabines brought their families. So the Roman males abducted the young women. The outraged Sabines went home and prepared for war. Meanwhile, Romulus reassured the Sabine women that they would enjoy the same rights as Roman women and be treated honorably. The men also managed to soothe their feelings with words of affection.

The Sabines and Latins combined against the Romans, and while the Latins retreated the Sabines took control of a Roman citadel by bribing a girl to let them enter and then killing her. The Sabines continued to march on the Romans but the two armies were saved from annihilating each other when the abducted women intervened and made them settle peacefully. From that time the two nations were united.

Commentary

The story of Aeneas was principally the creation of Vergil, although it had antecedents in the *Iliad* and in Roman legend. Vergil consciously modeled his tale on the two Homeric epics. The first half of *The Aeneid* is like *The Odyssey*, an account of a hero's wanderings, while the second half is like *The Iliad*, an account of war. But Vergil was uniquely original in portraying a hero who fights for a future civilization, not for his own honor or for any existing nation. Aeneas knows he bears a special destiny and he sacrifices much to fulfill it, abandoning site after site, leaving his newfound happiness with Dido, undertaking a terrible war, and finally killing the brave Turnus. Yet he is not ruthless, having a generous and compassionate heart. The difference between the way he kills Lausus and the way Turnus kills Pallas is the difference between a man with a great soul and a man who fights merely to win. It is precisely Aeneas' sense of mission that makes him morally superior, because he feels himself responsible for unborn generations of men. That sense of mission makes *The Aeneid* an original and outstanding work of Western culture. *The Iliad* by contrast is deeply pessimistic. Vergil affirms the life founded on hope and action while acknowledging life's sadness and the brutality of war.

The tale of Romulus and Remus, adapted here from Livy, is a mixture of folklore, mythical tradition, and invention. Romulus and Remus have a god for a father and a virgin for a mother; they are rescued miraculously; they grow up in humble circumstances; they battle with evildoers; and the secret of their parentage is revealed. Once Romulus gains his kingdom after killing Remus he rules wisely and capably, as effective in war as in peace. As a hero he is sufficient, but he lacks the transcendent stature of Aeneas.

Patriotic heroes were characteristic of Rome, for the Romans had a community spirit that elevated the idea of making personal sacrifices for the state. The Greeks lacked a sense of the common welfare and created individualistic heroes out for fame. In this respect the Romans represented an advance over Greek culture.

LOVE TALES

PYRAMUS AND THISBE

In Babylon there lived the most handsome pair of young lovers in the East. Pyramus loved Thisbe and she loved him, but although they were next-door neighbors they could never get together because both sets of parents opposed the courtship. In order to converse they had to whisper through a chink in the wall that separated them. Tired of this subterfuge, they agreed to meet one night outside the city to elope. Thisbe arrived at the meeting place under a mulberry tree and was frightened off by a lion with bloody jaws. The lion found her scarf and ripped it, staining the scarf with blood. When Pyramus came along he discovered the scarf and the lion's tracks and he assumed Thisbe had been killed. No longer wishing to live, he took his sword and plunged it into his body. The blood spurted upward and dyed the white mulberries red. Thisbe returned to find her lover at the point of death. She obtained his sword and committed suicide. The two of them were buried in a single urn. Since that time the mulberry tree has always put forth red berries.

BAUCIS AND PHILEMON

In Phrygia there grows an oak and a lime tree very close together beside a wall, and not far off is a wide marsh inhabited by birds. The story is this. The land was once peopled with an impious race who refused Jupiter and Mercury refuge when they came in disguise. The only couple that took the gods in was Baucis and Philemon, an elderly pair in very modest circumstances. Despite their poverty they treated Jupiter and Mercury with great hospitality, setting before them the best food they had. The wine cups mysteriously were refilled, and Baucis and Philemon knew they were in the presence of divinity then. The couple scrambled to kill their single goose for the gods, but the bird flew to the gods. Then Jupiter told the aged pair they must hurry up a nearby mountain because a flood was about to destroy their evil neighbors. Baucis and Philemon did so, accompanied by Jupiter and Mercury, and soon a flood swamped the countryside. Their own hut, however, was transformed before their eyes into a marble temple. The two gods offered to grant the couple anything they wished. They both requested to serve in the temple and to die at the same time, which the gods bestowed on them. After serving until it was time to die, Philemon suddenly found himself turning into an oak while Baucis was changed into a lime tree.

PYGMALION

Shunning the world of fickle women, Pygmalion thought it best to live singly. But being a sculptor he fashioned a dream woman, one very elegant, modest, and realistic. Obsessed with his own marble creation, he brought it gifts and even lay with it in bed. Although he knew it wasn't real, he was completely in love with his statue and longed for it to respond to him. At a festival dedicated to Venus, Pygmalion prayed to the goddess to give the statue life. He went home and embraced it, and as he did so a pulse began to beat and the marble turned to warm flesh in his arms. In this way Pygmalion achieved possession of his ideal woman.

VERTUMNUS AND POMONA

The nymph Pomona was single-mindedly devoted to the cultivation of fruit trees and, although she was strikingly beautiful, she disdained the suitors who flocked to her gardens and orchards. But one suitor was more determined than the rest. Vertumnus would resort to any disguise just to be near her—fisherman, farmer, shepherd. One day he visited her in the guise of an old woman and praised her fruit trees, kissing her passionately by way of greeting. The old woman then began to talk of her single state, of what a fine lad Vertumnus was, and of the dangers of rejecting men. She told Pomona a story of a young man who killed himself when rejected in love and of how the gods turned the woman who spurned him into a statue. But the words of the old woman did nothing to change Pomona. Finally in desperation Vertumnus threw off his disguise and stood naked before Pomona, who fell in love with his handsome form. They embraced and spent the rest of their lives tending fruit trees.

HERO AND LEANDER

In Sestus there lived the lovely Hero in a tower by the sea, where she ministered to Venus and Cupid. Across the Hellespont lived Leander, a striking young man. They met at a festival of Adonis and fell in love. Leander agreed to swim the Hellespont for an assignation with Hero, while Hero would light a lamp to guide him. Thus, during the summer the two enjoyed many secret nights of love. But winter came with fierce weather and Hero could not resist putting the lamp forth to guide Leander to her bed. He drowned in the attempt to swim across from Abydos to Sestus. When Hero looked down at the wave-battered rocks in the morning and saw his mangled body she plunged from a crag onto the rocks, uniting herself with Leander in death.

CUPID AND PSYCHE

A king had three daughters, of whom the youngest, Psyche, had such a radiant beauty that it rivaled Venus'. And people deserted the worship of Venus in adoration of Psyche. Venus was furious and commanded her son Cupid to make Psyche fall in love with the most loathsome creature on earth. However, Cupid, a handsome youth, fell in love with Psyche and asked Apollo for help. As time passed Psyche fell in love with no one, whereas her sisters were married to kings. Her parents consulted the oracle of Apollo, which commanded them to dress Psyche in mourning and take her to a rocky mount where a hideous and mighty dragon would carry her off to be its wife. Sadly her parents did as they were told and went home to mourn.

The gentle West Wind picked Psyche up and carried her off to a wondrous, fertile country. She awoke to find a palace of gold and silver and gems. Voices within the palace reassured her and she made herself welcome, bathing and eating. At night Cupid came to her in darkness and made love to her, but he left before daybreak. Even though she never saw him she knew he was godlike and handsome. Cupid would return every night, but happy as she was Psyche could not help thinking of her sisters, who were lamenting for her. Cupid warned her that her sisters would bring ruin, yet Psyche longed to see them. When at last they came to visit they were amazed and jealous to see Psyche's lavish wealth and to hear her speak so lovingly of her husband. When the sisters left, Cupid again warned Psyche of them, but since she had no other companions, she longed to see them. The sisters returned and made Psyche confess that she had never seen her husband. They made her doubt whether he was a man and not some hideous monster. Further, they gave her a knife to murder him and a lamp with which to see him. In her consternation Psyche decided to settle her husband's identity once and for all. In the night as Cupid lay asleep she brought the lighted lamp over to him with the dagger in her hand. But she saw the most handsome being alive on the bed and the dagger fell from her hand. But hot oil from the lamp fell on his shoulder. Awakening, he left her, but as he departed he revealed himself as the God of Love, who cannot live where trust is lacking.

Desolate, Psyche determined to find her husband and show him how strong her love really was. Cupid had returned to his mother Venus, but Venus was angry when she learned he had chosen Psyche. After praying to the gods in vain Psyche resolved to approach her arch-enemy Venus and offer to serve her humbly. It required all the courage Psyche could muster. And Venus received the girl with humiliating scorn, taunting her about her vanished husband. Venus observed that to obtain a mate such a plain-looking girl as Psyche must become accomplished in menial but diligent service. The goddess then set the poor girl an impossible task.

Psyche had to sort out a huge mixture of tiny seeds into separate piles. Bewildered at having to do it by nightfall Psyche was disheartened, but an army of ants felt compassion for her and sorted the seeds. Venus was angry when she found the job done, and she gave Psyche a bread crust and told her to sleep on the ground, thinking to destroy her beauty. The next morning Venus told the girl to fetch some of the golden fleece from very fierce sheep that grazed by a river. Psyche despaired of the task and considered drowning herself, but a reed advised her to wait till the sheep came out of the thicket near evening and she could gather the fleece from the thorns. Having accomplished it,

Psyche was given the task of fetching a vial of water from the source of the River Styx, which was unapproachable except by air. An eagle took the flask and filled it for her.

Then Venus gave Psyche a box to take to the underworld and borrow some of Proserpina's beauty. A tower told her how to reach the underworld and how to conduct hereself there, so Psyche safely passed Charon and Cerberus and reached the Queen of Death, who filled the box. As Psyche returned to Venus she was seized with curiosity to know what was in the box and thought to enhance her own beauty for Cupid's sake. As she opened the box and saw nothing in it she fell into a deathlike state.

By now Cupid had recovered from the wound that the hot oil had caused. Although Venus had locked him in his room, he escaped through a window and discovered Psyche in a swoon. Cupid took the sleep from her eyes, put it back in the box, and pricked her awake with an arrow. After reproaching her for her curiosity he assured her that everything would work out. As Psyche took the box to Venus, Cupid asked Jove to make Psyche immortal so that they might be officially married on Olympus. Jove consented, and the wedding took place. Venus no longer objected to the match, and they lived happily forever.

Commentary

These stories, as presented by Ovid, Musaeus, and Apuleius, are intended to entertain. The gods, who make appearances in some of these tales, are simply fictional devices, not religious beings. Here we see myth degenerated into yarn-spinning. Ovid's "Pyramus and Thisbe" and Musaeus' "Hero and Leander" show two sets of lovers that commit suicide. The purpose is sentimental, but the effect is bathetic, since each lover dies stupidly. Passion is inflated to grotesque proportions and utterly lacking in reason or prudence. In Ovid's "Pygmalion" love becomes pathological, morbid, as the hero idolatrizes his own statue after rejecting all real women. "Vertumnus and Pomona" is a silly treatment of the hardhearted woman with the ardent suitor theme, in which Ovid asserts the value of handsome nudity over fatuous persuasion. In each of these tales there is something effeminate and decadent. Ovid's "Baucis and Philemon" is a different matter, however. While it is sentimental it is touchingly so, for one feels affection for the humble elderly couple still very much in love.

Apuleius uses fairy tale motifs to suggest allegorical meanings in "Cupid and Psyche." There are the familiar devices of the serpent-human lover, the envious elder sisters, the magic prohibition, the wicked mother-in-law, the series of perilous tasks, the descent to the underworld, and the happy ending. Yet the story can be read as the soul's passage through hard discipline from carnal love to spiritual love. It also hints that a heavenly estate awaits the soul that patiently endures long trials in the service of love. Such ideas were not foreign to the cult of Isis, of which Apuleius was an initiate.

If the patriotic legend revealed the hard backbone of Roman culture, the love story tended to show its vulnerable belly. The elevation of passion into a ruling principle, the mixture of sentimentality and cynicism, the emphasis on metamorphoses and feminine psychology all suggest a decadent stage of civilization, a loss of nerve and vigor. Where erotic love excludes other realities it becomes effete and self-destructive. The tales of lovers who seal their union in death operate by this logic. The point is that when the old heroic legends lose their attraction one finds an obsession with love cropping up, and it means a culture has gone soft.

Norse Mythology

INTRODUCTION

Teutonic religion extended through Germany, Scandinavia, and England in the Dark Ages, and as Christianity supplanted it the old gods and rites were destroyed and forgotten. Much of our knowledge of this religion stems from *The Elder Edda* and *The Younger Edda,* which were compiled in Iceland during the Middle Ages. The *Eddas* project a stern and gloomy view of the cosmos and of man's role in it.

The world was created when Odin and his brothers slew the primeval Frost-Giant Ymir, and it will come to an end when the Giants rise against Odin and his comrades and kill them in battle. Certain doom awaits the gods and men alike, but in the face of that doom the one noble activity is war, and to die courageously fighting was the only way to enter Valhalla, the warrior's paradise. Love in the Norse tales was often accompanied by murderous passions, and treachery was commonplace. The world here is a hard, cold, bitter place in which to live.

Despite the starkness of this picture the Norsemen took intense pleasure from such things as friendship, drinking and eating, making love, outwitting strangers, avenging wrongs, and fighting bravely. They were a fierce, hard-headed race, and their myths take no pains to conceal it.

We will examine the creation and destruction of the universe, some tales of the gods, and the epic stories of *Beowulf,* the Volsungs, and Sigurd. These will give a more vivid and detailed version of how the Norsemen saw the world and what they valued.

SUPERNATURAL RACES IN NORSE MYTH

The *Aesir* were the primary race of gods, which included Odin, Thor, Tyr, Balder, and Heimdall, among others. They lived in Asgard and held temporary power over the cosmos. Aging like mortals, these gods renewed their youth by eating magic apples. Their reign would end and they would die at Ragnarok, when evil overcomes good in a final battle.

The ***Vanir*** were a secondary race of gods, not essentially different from the Aesir. In ancient times the Vanir and the Aesir battled one another until a compromise was reached in which the Vanir were admitted into Asgard. Among these gods were Frey and his beautiful sister Freya.

The ***Giants,*** whether Frost-Giants or Mountain-Giants, were terrible magicians who lived at Jötunheim, engaged in contests with the gods, and would shatter the cosmos at Ragnarok.

The ***Dwarves*** were a subterranean race of craftsmen.

The ***Valkyries,*** "choosers of the slain," were female warriors who selected brave mortal fighters who died in battle to live in Valhalla in Asgard. Attendants of Odin, the Valkyries were also immortal waitresses that refilled the drinking cups in Valhalla. They were visible only to men about to die fighting.

THE MAJOR NORSE GODS

Odin (Woden, Wotan) was the chief god, a master of wisdom, magic, and poetry. A protector of courageous noblemen in war, he was also the god of the slain. Odin was blind in one eye, wore a golden breastplate and helmet, carried a magic spear, and rode an incredibly swift, eight-legged horse named Sleipnir. On his shoulders perched two ravens, Hugin and Munin (thought and memory), that flew throughout the world and reported everything to him each night.

Frigga was Odin's wife, who was also wise. She protected brave warriors whom Odin neglected. Both Frigga and Odin had extramarital sexual encounters.

Thor was the god of thunder, a powerful deity, upright in character but fearsome to his enemies. He protected peasant warriors and possessed a belt that doubled his strength, iron gloves, and a magic hammer, Mjölnir, which always struck its target and returned to Thor's hand.

Balder, the son of Odin and Frigga, was especially favored and loved by nearly every being in the world, but he was the first god to die, killed by Loki's treachery.

Tyr presided over public assemblies, legal matters, and battles. His hand was bitten off by Fenrir the wolf, a monstrous enemy of the gods.

Frey was the god of vegetation and fertility.

Freya, his sister, was the goddess of love and beauty.

Heimdall was the watchman of the gods, stationed on the rainbow bridge, Bifröst, that led to Asgard. His trumpet would announce doomsday.

Loki, although allowed in Asgard, was the son of a Giant. Full of malice and cunning, he perpetrated much mischief until the gods bound him in a cavern with a venomous serpent to torment him. He fathered three mighty monsters, including Fenrir the wolf and the Midgard Serpent.

Hel was goddess of the netherworld, and half her face had human features while the other half was blank. She ruled the dead.

CREATION AND CATASTROPHE

At first there was only a great void. But to the North of this void there formed a region of mist and ice, while to the South grew a region of fire. Niflheim was the name of the North, and Muspellsheim of the South; and the heat from the latter melted some of the ice of the former, which shaped Ymir, the Frost-Giant with a human form. From Ymir's sweat came the race of Giants, and as the glacial ice melted further a huge cow was created to feed the Giants. This cow in turn was fed by salt contained in the ice. One day it licked the ice and hair emerged, on the next day a head, and on the third day Bur emerged, fully formed. Bur had a son, Buri, who had three sons—Odin, Vili, and Ve. These three were a new race, not Giants but gods. They banded together and murdered Ymir. Most of the other Giants drowned in Ymir's blood, which created a great sea. From Ymir's body the three gods made solid land, the earth, and from Ymir's skull they made the vault of the heavens. Odin and his brothers then created the race of dwarves from the maggots in Ymir's body. Other gods joined these three, and together they erected Asgard and all its halls to be their own home.

Having established their supremacy, the gods made the first mortals, shaping a man from an ash tree and a woman from a vine. The gods bestowed breath, energy, a soul, reason, warmth, and freshness on this first couple. And from their male descendants Odin chose only the bravest to live in Asgard after they died, for these warriors would aid him in the final showdown with the forces of evil.

The cosmos was supported by a tremendous ash tree, Yggdrasil. One of its roots extended to Niflheim, which was the netherworld; another to Jötunheim, the dwelling place of Giants; another to Midgard, the home of man; and one to Asgard, the home of the gods. In its upper branches lived a squirrel and an eagle, while at its rootage lived the serpent Nidhögg, which gnawed away, until at the end of time the whole structure would collapse. In the meantime the Norns, or Fates, watered the tree to keep it from dying.

Odin knew the power of the gods was not eternal, for he and his comrades would die when the Giants and demons rose against them. The last fight would take place at Vigrid, a field one hundred miles in length and breadth. Odin would be swallowed by Fenrir the wolf, but his son would avenge him. Thor and the Midgard Serpent would destroy each other; so would Loki and Heimdall; and Tyr would slay Garm, the fierce dog of Niflheim, and be clawed to death in turn. The stars and all heavenly bodies would plummet from the sky as the earth sank beneath the sea. The twilight of the gods would become night, and the universe would exist no more.

Yet there still existed a power, the Nameless One, that would give birth to a new world beyond the edge of time.

ODIN

From the first Odin had a desire for knowledge and wisdom, and he consulted all living things to obtain them. He gained most from his uncle Mimir, who guarded the Well of Knowledge, but he had to sacrifice an eye to drink from the Well. Odin also went to great lengths to acquire the art of poetry, which was contained in a magic potion that was kept in a Giant's underground caldron. Having determined to obtain the potion, Odin put himself in bondage to a Giant, whom he persuaded to blast a hole to the underground dwelling where the substance was kept. Odin then entered the dwelling as a snake, changed back into human shape, made friends with Suttung the Giant, who owned the potion, seduced the Giant's daughter, and obtained the mixture from her. Then he flew back to Asgard as an eagle, destroying Suttung in the process, and dispensed the potion to human poets.

The gods were subject to aging, and they rejuvenated themselves by eating magic apples kept by the goddess Idun. However, Odin chose a different, harder way. He freely wounded himself with his own spear and hung himself for nine days from the cosmic tree Yggdrasil, which was shaken by winds. In this manner he renewed his youth, but he also became the master of the magic runes, inscriptions that could accomplish any mortal purpose, whether beneficial or baneful.

Through his powers of wisdom, poetry, and magic Odin was of much use to men. In warfare his mere presence could strike the enemy blind, deaf, and impotent. He valued courage above all other human traits, a quality which he himself possessed in abundance. Fully aware that he himself, his followers and comrades, and the universe itself were doomed, bravery was what mattered most to him in the face of certain defeat. Thus he collected a band of only the most courageous warriors to sit with him in Valhalla. These men would go down fighting with him at the crack of destruction. And Odin would be devoured by the wolf Fenrir.

THOR

The god of storm and thunder, Thor was a mighty fighter. He had iron gloves, a girdle that doubled his power, and an invincible flying hammer. Thor traveled in a chariot drawn by male goats. When he was hungry he killed and ate them, but he simply laid his hammer on their hides to revive them. One day Thor discovered that his hammer was missing, and Loki found that the Giant Thrym had stolen it. Thrym wanted to marry Freya in return for the hammer, but the goddess Freya loathed the idea. So it was decided that Thor would go to Thrym's hall disguised as Freya. Thor took Loki with him. Thrym was astonished at how much the bride ate and drank, but Loki told him "she" had not eaten or drunk for nine days in her anxiousness to join the Giants. Thrym then went to kiss his bride and was amazed that she had a red complexion and eyes that flashed fire. Again Loki explained she was feverish from lack of sleep in her joy at joining Thrym. In a hurry to get the marriage over with, Thrym ordered that the hammer be placed on the bride's knees according to custom. Thor laughted in his heart, and having regained his hammer he struck all the Giants in the hall dead.

Resolved to kill the Midgard Serpent that surrounded the earth, ate its own tail, and lived in the ocean, Thor accepted shelter from the Giant Hymir. When Thor said he wished to go fishing, Hymir treated him contemptuously. But Thor slew one of Hymir's bulls to use the head for bait, and he and Hymir sailed out into the ocean. Thor took the boat far past the point that Hymir felt was safe. Then he baited the hook and threw it in the sea. Before long the Midgard Serpent snatched the bait and was caught. Its thrashing banged up Thor's hands and wrists against the gunwale, and in the struggle the bottom of the boat fell through, so that Thor found himself standing on the ocean floor. With that added stability he drew the serpent up with an enormous heave. As he was about to slay the monster with his hammer the terrified Hymir cut the line, allowing the serpent to escape. Thor then felled and drowned the cowardly Hymir as he tried to escape. But he would not kill the Midgard Serpent till doomsday, or Ragnarok, when he would perish as well.

Thor could be tricked by magic. After a long day's travel with Loki and two peasants in the land of the Giants, Thor came to an odd house in which the front door was as wide as the dwelling itself. During the night earthquakes and rumblings forced them from the house into an adjacent shed. When morning came Thor found a sleeping Giant nearby whose snorings and heavings shook the ground. The Giant awoke, told Thor his name was Skrymir, revealed their shelter had been his glove, and offered to accompany the group. Skrymir carried the sack of provisions, and that night when the group sat down to eat the sack could not be opened. Skrymir lay asleep, and in a fury Thor hurled his hammer at the Giant, who awoke and said he felt a leaf had fallen on him. Thor flung his hammer even harder, and this time Skrymir thought he had been hit by an acorn. Utterly enraged, Thor flung the hammer with all his might, only to find that Skrymir thought he had been awakened by bird droppings. Skrymir took his leave of Thor and his comrades the next morning after pointing out their destination, Utgard, and telling them there were tougher fellows than he at Utgard.

Thor, Loki, and the two peasants came to a fortress and had to squeeze through the grilled doorway to enter. There they encountered King Utgardaloki surrounded by Giants. Utgardaloki addressed them scornfully and challenged them to prove their skill in a contest with the Giants present. Loki boasted that he could eat great quantities of food quickly, but in an eating competition with Logi, Loki only devoured a platterful of meat while Logi ate the meat, bones, and plate. Thor's companion, a peasant, said he was swift as lightning and proved it in a race, but his competitor Hugi still outdistanced him. Thor claimed he could drink more than any being alive, but after taking enormous quaffs from a drinking horn the level of liquid was only a small degree lower. Then Utgardaloki tested Thor's strength by having him lift a cat from the floor, but Thor could do no more than lift a paw or two. Finally Thor agreed to wrestle an old woman, and the old woman brought him to one knee. Utgardaloki then gave an account of every humiliating thing that had happened to Thor and his friends, saying that their strength was truly frightening. He himself had been Skrymir, and if he had not protected his head with mountains Thor's hammer would have killed him. Instead, those mountains now had deep ridges. Loki had eaten in a contest with Logi—fire—which devours everything. The peasant had raced with Hugi—thought—the swiftest medium. Thor had drunk from the sea and lowered it a few inches, had tried to lift the Midgard Serpent, and had wrestled with old age. Infuriated at having played the fool, Thor lifted his hammer to slay the enchanter, but Utgardaloki and his castle vanished, leaving Thor and his comrades alone on the plain.

BALDER

Balder was the most glorious god alive, handsome and pure in spirit, the son of Odin and Frigga. Every living creature loved him. Yet Odin knew his son was doomed to an early death. To protect him Frigga traveled far and wide, exacting promises from all objects and beings not to harm him. Believing she had done everything possible, Frigga neglected the lowly mistletoe. The gods rejoiced to know that Balder was invulnerable and invented a game in which everyone threw things at him.

Loki was intensely jealous of Balder and resolved to destroy him. While all the gods hurled things at Balder, Balder's blind brother Hoder sat by himself, unable to join the fun. Loki, having learned the secret of the mistletoe and having obtained a sprig, offered to guide the blind Hoder's hand. The mistletoe was thrown and it pierced Balder's heart, killing him. The gods grieved, but Odin and Frigga sent another son as an envoy to the underworld, Niflheim, to see if Balder could be ransomed. In the meantime Balder's funeral ship was prepared, set fire to, and sent out to sea.

The goddess Hel agreed to release Balder from her kingdom of death only if the whole creation and everything in it wept for the slain god. Messengers were sent everywhere, and all things cried over Balder's death until one messenger came upon a Giantess who refused to weep. This of course was Loki in disguise. So Balder was condemned to remain in the netherworld. But the gods revenged themselves on Loki by binding him in a deep cave and causing a poisonous serpent to drip venom in his face, causing the wicked being intolerable pain. Loki's wife caught much of this venom in a cup, but whenever she emptied the cup Loki writhed in agony, creating earthquakes.

This was the beginning of the end, for Loki then allied himself with the Giants and demons, who would bring ruin on the Aesir.

FREY

A god of fertility, vegetation, and sailing, Frey was one of the beneficial Vanir admitted into Asgard. Once Frey sat on Odin's high throne watching the earth. He became enamored of a Giant's beautiful daughter, Gerda, and determined to have her as his wife. His friend and servant Skirnir agreed to woo Gerda for him. Taking Frey's wondrous sword and fearless horse, Skirnir braved the dangers of reaching the Giant's dwelling, even riding through a wall of flame. Gerda was not in the least impressed with Skirnir, though he offered her rich gifts. Then he threatened her and her father with the sword to no avail. However, when Skirnir vowed to turn her into a withered, desolate old maid, Gerda capitulated and said she would marry Frey in nine days. Frey, impatient for the nine days to elapse, won his bride in this manner.

FREYA

Also one of the Vanir, Freya had stunning beauty, and she loved to adorn herself with jewelry. In the workshop of four dwarves Freya discovered a lovely golden necklace that she desired. She offered the dwarves much wealth for it, but they wanted her to sleep with each of them for a night instead. Freya consented. But Odin disapproved of her actions and ordered Loki to steal the necklace. That evening Loki found it impossible to enter Freya's dwelling, so he changed himself into a fly and entered through a chink in the roof. Since she was wearing the necklace and it was impossible to remove without disturbing her, Loki became a flea and bit her, causing Freya to shift. Loki then resumed his human form, took the necklace and left. When she awoke she knew Odin had the necklace, so she went to him. But Odin agreed to return it only if she created a war between two great kings with twenty kings apiece under their command, and if each night she would restore the slain warriors to life. The war took place and Freya recovered her precious necklace.

LOKI

The god of wiles and wickedness, Loki was very handsome and had enjoyed the favors of many goddesses. One of his last dramatic exploits concerned the feast of Aegir, a Giant and lord of the sea. Aegir had invited all the gods and goddesses to attend. Thor was not present, but the other deities were having a grand time when Loki forced his way into the hall. Knowing his malicious trickery, the gods did not welcome him. But Loki appealed to the rules of hospitality and his pledge with Odin, and very reluctantly the gods made a place for him and gave him drink. Then Loki began attacking the gods and goddesses, one by one, telling of their infidelities, their cowardices, the times they had been made to look foolish, all the tricks with which he had humiliated them. Any attempts at reconciliation were met with scurrilous abuse. And when others offered him insult for insult Loki outdid them in contempt. Odin himself was nonplussed. When the feast was in a thorough uproar Thor returned, fierce and commanding. And Loki reminded Thor of his adventure with Utgardaloki. Thor brandished his hammer, which made Loki cower. But before he left the banquet he warned that that would be the last feast they would attend, for soon Aegir's hall and the entire world would be burning.

Commentary

Several days of our week are named after the Teutonic gods: Tuesday after Tyr, Wednesday after Odin (Woden), Thursday after Thor, and Friday after Frey. The mythological stories of the Norse gods show a culture that centered on warfare, and these gods are glorified human warriors who get their way by force, by magic, and by cunning. Balder and, in part, Odin show a certain amount of spirituality; yet on the whole the Norse gods are not very elevating, as Loki points out at Aegir's feast. These are gods who are doomed and know it, and like many men they are determined to get all the pleasure they can from life before they die. Courage, strength, and cleverness are what count to them.

Despite their moral laxity, however, the Aesir were regarded as the noblest beings in existence. They supported human civilization, such as it was, against the titanic destructive forces in nature such as the Giants and demons. In the frozen world of Scandinavia such beings were necessary to the primitive culture; and survival depended on fighting for the little land there was. Yet war seemed to become an end in itself, the main justification for living. Heroism in such a world becomes self-destructive and meaningless. To fight for the sheer joy of fighting is a terrible waste, like suicide. Despite the excesses to which the Teutonic religion tended, the Norse gods have a certain gloomy grandeur.

BEOWULF

A distant descendant of the great warrior Scyld, King Hrothgar of Denmark wanted to create something that would make his name imperishable. So he built an enormous mead hall for himself and his earls, one larger than any before it. This was Heorot Hall, where fine bards sang for the king and his men. A curse soon fell on Hrothgar's kingdom. The fiendish ogre Grendel, a monster from the fens, ravaged the land. He was mighty and had a hairy, stinking hide that no weapon could penetrate. Time after time he charged into Heorot Hall, slaughtered the earls like sheep, and feasted on them. Hrothgar alone was exempt, for Grendel was forbidden to touch the king. This lasted twelve years, since nothing could stop the ogre. Denmark trembled in fear and grief.

The Geatish king Hygelac heard of the trouble. Among Hygelac's earls was the invincible Beowulf, son of Ecgtheow, a hero who wished to kill Grendel. Taking fifteen bold comrades, Beowulf sailed for Denmark. Arriving safely, they were greeted by an awestruck earl who led the company to Heorot Hall, where Beowulf made himself known to the herald. Led into Hrothgar's presence, Beowulf greeted the king and told him of his perilous mission. Hrothgar lamented his own old age and weakness in the face of bloody Grendel, but he welcomed Beowulf and his men heartily.

At evening, merriment filled the great mead hall after its long desolation. Unferth, one of Hrothgar's earls, was envious of Beowulf and tried to bait him, claiming that Beowulf had been beaten in a swimming contest. But Beowulf had not only won the contest, he had survived a terrible storm after five days and nights of swimming and had killed a sea-monster as well. And now he had come to slay Grendel. Queen Wealhtheow greeted Beowulf warmly, and King Hrothgar offered the hero anything he wished if he should kill the fiend.

That night as the warriors lay asleep Grendel shattered the bolted door, killed a man, and ate of him. Glaring around the hall he spotted Beowulf and sprang at him. Beowulf caught the ogre's right hand and stopped his charge. Grendel was shaken with fear as Beowulf twisted his arm. He tried violently to break loose but the hero held on. Warriors cowered from the terrific struggle, yet one of Beowulf's men tried to cut Grendel down but could not succeed. As Grendel shrieked Beowulf wrenched his arm to the breaking point and finally snapped the whole thing off. The dying Grendel burst out into the night. And Beowulf nailed the trophy to the rafters of Heorot Hall.

News spread quickly of the hero's deed. Songs were written of it, and people gawked at Beowulf. Denmark rejoiced. Hrothgar treated Beowulf as a son, presenting him and his comrades with many gifts. However, Grendel's mother, a demoness, was enraged at her son's death. The next night she stole into Heorot Hall and killed Hrothgar's closest friend. She put the place in an uproar but escaped easily, taking Grendel's arm.

The next morning Hrothgar summoned Beowulf from his neighboring lodge to tell him of the ogress and her treachery. The king also told Beowulf of her lair deep in a frightful tarn not far off. The hero agreed to pursue the hag, and warriors accompanied him to the hellish site. They saw sea-monsters swimming under the waves, so Beowulf killed one with his lance. Then he donned his armor and plunged into the inlet. For hours he swam downward. The ogress saw him and caught him in her claws about his waist. Failing to pierce his armor, she drew him ever deeper past grotesque fish that cut his thighs, down to her underground cavern. In the cave there was air from which he drew breath and a harsh light. He swung his sword, Hrunting, against Grendel's mother but it bent and chipped. In the scuffle Beowulf realized he was no match for the ogress, who would have killed him if he had not seen the fabled sword of the Giants on the cave wall. He seized it and swung, slaying his savage opponent. A golden light then filled the cavern, revealing the dead Grendel. Beowulf cut his head off, looking longingly at the hoard of wealth, but left it behind as he swam to the surface with Grendel's head.

On reaching the surface, he found only his own companions waiting for him, since Hrothgar and his men had left, assuming he was dead. Beowulf and his troop of Geats marched back to Hrothgar with the severed head. Hrothgar, of course, was overjoyed now that Beowulf and Denmark were safe. He gave the Geats more rich gifts. Yet before Beowulf sailed back to his homeland Hrothgar warned him of being proud, for that fault could bring any great warrior to ruin.

Back in his homeland Beowulf gave all his new wealth to his uncle, King Hygelac. Even though Beowulf's prowess, generosity, and courtesy were much praised, the envious spoke evil of him. However, Hygelac rewarded Beowulf with land. When Hygelac fell in battle with the Frisians many felt Beowulf should have had the throne after he defeated the Frisians, but he supported Hygelac's successor. When that king died Beowulf took the throne and ruled virtuously and prudently for fifty years. Then a dragon rose against the Geats. Some man had stolen a golden cup from the dragon's hoard of wealth and used it to buy his freedom. In retaliation the great worm burned dwellings all along the coast and left nothing alive.

Old Beowulf was angered and grieved. He decided to meet the dragon in single combat, and had steel armor made to protect him from the monster's flaming mouth. Then he took thirteen earls to the cliff that overhung the dragon and his hoard. Among these was the man who had stolen the golden cup, whom Beowulf brought to point out the hidden passage to the dragon's nest. Before descending through the passage to meet the beast, Beowulf reminisced about his own life and deeds and what he had seen. He vowed to grapple with the winged serpent alone and made his way through the rock to its lair

As he challenged the dragon it sent a stream of fire at his legs and uncoiled to attack. Beowulf's sword was useless against the great worm, which scorched the hero's body mercilessly. From above the earls saw that Beowulf was losing, and all but one cowered. That was Wiglaf, who reproached his companions for their cowardice and strode down to aid the gallant old king. Wiglaf stood beside his leader and told him to retreat, but Beowulf could not hear. The serpent burned away Wiglaf's shield and armor, yet Wiglaf stood his ground behind Beowulf's steel shield. Taking courage from Wiglaf's presence, Beowulf assaulted the dragon with a second sword, but that melted too. The monster charged again, coming within inches of Beowulf's face and gouging into his neck with its claws. Meanwhile, Wiglaf kept jabbing at the serpent's belly, which lessened its fire, allowing Beowulf to strike one last blow with his dagger, a blow that finished the dragon for good.

But Beowulf by now was nearly dead as the dragon's poison crept through his body. Wiglaf dressed the king's wounds, and Beowulf asked to see some of the monster's hoard. Then Beowulf willed the hoard to his people and requested that a funeral mound be built on the cliff above to serve as a beacon for ships. Lastly, he passed the tokens of kingship over to Wiglaf, his successor. The other earls finally came from their hiding places, and Wiglaf declared them outcasts.

The Geats mourned Beowulf's death, for he had been a great king. Now it was likely they would be invaded and enslaved by their enemies. That Beowulf should die because one man had taken a cup was tragic, and so the Geats buried the hoard with curses, never to be unearthed. And as a memorial to their dead king they built a lighthouse over his burial pile on the cliff. The wise and mighty Beowulf would also be remembered in song.

THE VOLSUNGS

Odin fathered Sigi and at times bestowed favors on Sigi's descendants. When Sigi's son, Rerir, proved childless, Odin gave Rerir's wife an apple and in a short time she gave birth to Volsung, who became a powerful warrior. Among Volsung's children were Signy and Sigmund. Signy married a foreigner, Hunding, a treacherous man with no love for his in-laws.

One day the Volsungs were holding a banquet in their hall when a stranger appeared in a wide-brimmed hat and a large cloak. A gleaming sword was in his hand, and the stranger plunged it into the large tree that supported the rafters. He announced that the person to pull it out should own it, and then he vanished. It was Odin in disguise. Everyone tried to extract it and failed until Sigmund tried and wrenched it free.

Somehow Hunding managed to make captives of all the Volsungs, including Sigmund. Night after night he chained them outside, where they were devoured by wolves. At last only Sigmund was left. His desperate sister Signy, torn between her family and conjugal loyalties, freed Sigmund and brought him the wondrous sword he had won. She also slept with Sigmund to give him a son necessary to avenge the murder of their kin. When the son was an infant she secretly gave him to her brother Sigmund to raise. This was Sigurd, born to be as fine a hero as his father. When Sigurd was grown he and Sigmund returned to avenge Hunding's bloody deeds. After imprisoning Hunding in his hall, they set fire to it. Signy watched enraptured now that her kin had destroyed the evildoer, but Hunding was still her husband, and she rushed into the burning hall to perish with him.

Sigmund performed many marvelous deeds of war with Odin's sword, but the time came that Odin had appointed for him to die. In the middle of a battlefield Sigmund saw the same figure that had entered his father's hall long years before. Odin touched the sword with his wooden staff and it broke in two. Sigmund was then mortally wounded by the foe. His wife tried to save him, but he calmly accepted Odin's will, knowing he would enter Valhalla. Yet he requested that the fabulous sword be allowed to be joined back together for another hero, which Odin granted.

SIGURD

That hero was Sigmund's son, Sigurd. He discovered the two pieces of the sword and had the dwarves forge them together. He had heard of the sleeping Valkyrie Brynhild, who was surrounded by a ring of fire that only a fearless warrior could break through. Brynhild had been punished by Odin for disobedience, and Sigurd resolved to rescue her. His search was long and perilous. During it he met and slew the dragon Fafnir, thereby obtaining the pile of gold and gems which the beast guarded. He also met an old wise man who revealed his future: Sigurd would prove the bravest of heroes, do nothing base, and yet his end would be full of wrath and anguish.

Arriving at the wall of flame Sigurd rode his horse through and awakened Brynhild, who gave herself to him in delight. He remained several days with her, only to leave her in that place. Sigurd traveled to the Giukungs, who were ruled by Gunnar, a king with whom he swore brotherhood. Gunnar had a sorceress for a mother—Griemhild—and she arranged it that Sigurd forgot Brynhild and married her daughter Gudrun. Sigurd had intended to retrieve Brynhild for himself, but having no memory of her he now undertook to win her for Gunnar, who was lacking in bravery. With Griemhild's magic he assumed Gunnar's form and passed again through the wall of flame. When he lay with Brynhild this time there was a sword between them, a token of Sigurd's loyalty to Gunnar and Gudrun. Brynhild now felt that Sigurd had deserted her, so she rode off to Gunnar's kingdom with this strange hero.

Back in Gunnar's land Sigurd secretly resumed his true form, and Brynhild was married to Gunnar. Brynhild resented Sigurd for his faithlessness. But resentment flared to hatred when, in a bitter quarrel with Gudrun, she learned that it had actually been Sigurd who had rescued her, rather than Gunnar. She wanted a dire revenge. To fan Gunnar's jealousy and injured pride Brynhild told him that Sigurd had possessed her for three nights, when they had really slept with the sword between them. She also told Gunnar that he must kill Sigurd or she would desert him. But Gunnar could not do it, for it would break his oath of brotherhood. Instead, Gunnar had a younger brother kill Sigurd as he slept.

Brynhild laughed bitterly as she heard Gudrun's shrieks on finding herself covered with her husband's blood. The Valkyrie told her anguished husband that Sigurd had remained pure and loyal, that her own love was given totally to Sigurd, and that she would die on his funeral pyre. Gudrun herself could not weep over her husband's murder. She sat silently beside the shroud, and others feared for her life. The women told stories of the terrible things that had happened to them in their lives, but Gudrun remained stony. At last one old woman uncovered Sigurd's head and laid it in Gudrun's lap to kiss. On seeing the bloody, lifeless face of Sigurd, Gudrun's stony reserve dissolved in tears.

Commentary

These three stories present a dark but accurate picture of how the Norsemen viewed human life. All men, even the strongest and noblest, are fated to unhappiness. Sorrow is man's one sure heritage, and the best way to meet it is to grapple with it courageously, in one's bare hands so to speak, as the aged Beowulf met the dragon. This quality of risking one's whole life in combat gave the Norsemen a special vibrancy. At its best, in Beowulf, it could be truly ennobling. Beowulf accomplished his feats of monster-killing to help others, and whatever wealth he gained from them he gave away. His unselfishness made him an exemplary king and hero.

At its worst the fighting instinct came down to mere tribalism, as in the tale of the Volsungs. Hunding and Sigmund are of different tribes, and in the animosity between them any cruelty is justified. Signy, of course, is caught between them. And while she does everything possible to avenge the murders of her family, she also decides in the end to die with her husband. This story underscores the ferocity of tribal loyalty.

The legend of Sigurd demonstrates how a notable and courageous warrior is brought low by the cunning and malice of women who want him for selfish reasons. Yet even these women have a somber dignity. They are not ignoble, merely intensely passionate. Sigurd is trapped between Brynhild and Gudrun and he falls victim to their jealousy.

In Norse myth there are no happy endings, because the Teutonic races saw the world as harsh, bleak, cold, with inexorable laws. That gloomy outlook persists today in Scandinavia and northern Germany, although it has been Christianized.

Arthurian Legends

INTRODUCTION

It seems possible that King Arthur was an actual person, a Welsh chieftain who lived around 500 A.D., a century after the Romans had withdrawn from Britain. Welsh writers kept his memory alive until in the twelfth century Geoffrey of Monmouth wrote *History of the Kings of Britain,* which established Arthur once and for all as a permanent part of European culture. From then on writers in England and on the Continent told of Arthur and his knights. By the time Malory wrote his *Morte d'Arthur* in the fifteenth century Arthur was considered one of the Nine Worthies, on a par with King David, Alexander the Great, and Charlemagne. Our account derives from Malory, Geoffrey, the Welsh *Mabinogeon, Sir Gawain and the Green Knight,* and *Parzival,* for the most part.

The primary source of Arthurian legend is the medieval romance, a digressive literary form in which knights, ladies, evildoers, magic, miracles, combats, tournaments, and quests provide the interest. The crude warrior code of the Dark Ages is sublimated here, thanks largely to the Church, and put in the service of a grand ideal. Religion and love are the new factors that turn warfare away from mere tribal butchery into a fight for abstract principles. King Arthur and his knights became the embodiment of the chivalric code, and in these legends we will see the driving force behind that code.

MERLIN

King Vortigern's fortress in Snowdon kept tumbling each night after expert masons had worked on it. His wizards advised him to find a youth that never had a father and sprinkle his blood on the foundations. After looking throughout Britain Vortigern's men found such a youth in Wales, Merlin. In Vortigern's court Merlin's mother testified that Merlin's father had been a spirit, an incubus. In the face of imminent death Merlin appeared unafraid. He told the king that an underground lake prevented the fortress from standing. When he had given directions for the draining of the lake Merlin prophesied that two dragons lay asleep on the bottom, a red one and a white one. The dragons were duly found, and they awoke and began fighting. The red dragon won. Vortigern asked what this meant, and Merlin told him he would soon be defeated and killed. Ambrosius landed the next day and proceeded to conquer Britain.

Merlin retired from public view until King Ambrosius wanted to build a great memorial. Ambrosius sent for the magician, who advised him to obtain the Dance of Giants stones from Ireland. Ambrosius' brother, Uther Pendragon, then defeated the Irish. With Merlin's help the huge stones were taken back to England and set up at Stonehenge. With the memorial completed, Merlin saw a blazing star in the shape of a dragon, an omen foretelling Ambrosius' death, the kingship of Uther Pendragon, and a future king—Uther's son—who would prove to be the greatest sovereign Britain would ever have.

At King Uther's coronation feast he fell in love with Ygraine, the wife of Gorlois, the Duke of Cornwall. Scandalously he showered her with attention, until Gorlois took Ygraine and his troops back to Cornwall and prepared for war. The heart-stricken Uther called his council, which advised him to call Gorlois back to court. If he refused to come Uther should lay siege to Cornwall, and that is what occurred. Uther trapped Gorlois in the castle Dimilioc, whereas Ygraine was at Tintagel, an impregnable castle. The king finally turned to Merlin for help. By magic Merlin turned Uther into the likeness of Gorlois. He also changed himself and another into likenesses of Gorlois' comrades. By this strategem they gained access to Tintagel, where Uther slept with Ygraine, who conceived Arthur that night. The next morning news arrived that Gorlois had been slain in battle the previous day. Uther confessed to the imposture and married Ygraine shortly thereafter.

Uther had promised Merlin that he might have the infant born to Ygraine. So when Arthur was born he was handed over to Merlin, who placed him with the knight Sir Ector. Merlin tutored the boy, and at the age of fifteen Arthur became the king of Britain. King Uther had left no other male heirs. Arthur took Merlin as his adviser, aide, and soothsayer, and the wizard foretold much that would happen to Arthur.

In his old age Merlin fell hopelessly in love with a young woman, Vivian, to whom he taught all the secrets of magic in return for her love. After learning his magical arts the thankless girl cast a spell on him that left Merlin imprisoned in a tower or a cave. Merlin will awaken, however, when King Arthur rises again to lead Britain through a period of her greatest peril.

KING ARTHUR

Arthur was reared by Sir Ector, whom he believed to be his natural father. King Uther had died in the meantime and for years Britain was torn by feuds over the kingship. Bishop Brice prayed one Christmas for a means by which a king might be chosen. Immediately a sword stuck in an anvil placed in a stone block appeared in the churchyard. An inscription read that the person to pull the sword loose would be king. So all the nobles tried and failed.

Sir Ector brought his son, Sir Kay, and his foster son, Arthur, to the London festivities. Sir Kay had left his sword at home and sent his squire, Arthur, to fetch it. Finding the place locked, Arthur remembered the sword in the churchyard and went to get it. He pulled it from the anvil easily and presented it to Sir Kay, who recognized it and claimed to be the new king. However, Sir Ector forced his son to confess that Arthur had given him the sword. After Arthur had replaced the sword in the anvil it was conclusively proved that only he could remove it. The commoners and many nobles accepted Arthur as king, and he was duly crowned. He generously made Sir Kay his steward.

Yet a number of nobles refused to accept this fifteen-year-old as their rightful king. So Arthur had to fight to establish his kingship. Arthur set up a court at Caerleon and one at Camelot. Six hostile leaders laid siege to Caerleon, but Arthur and his troops drove them off. But these enemy kings were joined by five more kings, and together they raised an army of sixty thousand. Arthur sent to Brittany and Gaul for support, which helped reduce the odds against him. The two armies met at Rockingham, where Merlin caused the enemy tents to collapse at night, which allowed the Arthurian forces to rush in and attack. The next day the fighting was ferocious, but Arthur managed to win the battle through superior strategy and bravery. Once the eleven kings had been routed Arthur turned his attention to the Saxons that had been invading Britain for years. Again, Arthur received aid from Brittany and met the Saxons at Mount Badon, where he and his troops were greatly outnumbered once more. Splendidly armored, Arthur charged the Saxons after a prayer to the Virgin Mary. He created havoc among the coarse barbarians, and victory was his again.

Having secured his kingdom, Arthur undertook expeditions against the Scots, Picts, Irish, Icelanders, Norwegians, and the Gauls. All of these campaigns were victorious. He thereby became the chief king of Christendom, while foreign courts imitated the styles at Camelot. Only once during the rest of Arthur's reign did a foreign power—Rome—try to exact tribute from him, but Rome paid dearly for such presumption.

In the meanwhile Arthur was attracting many noblemen as knights to his court. Among these was Gawain, who came with his mother, Morgause. Although Morgause was married to King Lot, one of Arthur's enemies, she fell in love with the young king and conceived a child by him. Unwittingly Arthur had slept with his own half sister, the daughter of Ygraine and Gorlois. From this incestuous and adulterous union came Modred, the evil knight that would destroy Arthur and his court. Arthur learned the secret of his true parentage after that amorous encounter.

Arthur acquired his famous sword, Excalibur, in this way. He saved Merlin from three murderous rogues, and Merlin accompanied him to the wood where King Pellinore, a knight, was challenging all passersby. While Arthur was a brave, capable fighter, he was overmatched by King Pellinore, who was mighty and experienced in single combat. Arthur's sword broke and he was badly wounded. Pellinore knocked Arthur unconscious while wrestling and was about to slay him when Merlin cast a spell that put Pellinore to sleep. Arthur awoke and Merlin took him to a hermit who healed his wounds. Then Merlin and Arthur rode to a lake, in the middle of which was a hand clasping an upraised sword. A maiden in a small boat appeared and told Arthur that he could have the sword if he would grant her a request later. Arthur agreed, got into the boat and fetched the sword, Excalibur, which was encased in a jeweled scabbard. Thus Arthur obtained his fabulous sword from the Lady of the Lake. But as Merlin pointed out, the scabbard was more valuable, since while Arthur wore it his wounds would not bleed. On returning to his court, Arthur found that his knights respected him even more for undertaking an adventure like an ordinary knight.

Arthur won his wife, Guinevere, in another risky undertaking. Riding with Merlin and a company of knights to Carmalide, Arthur found King Laodegan besieged by the Irish. The Irish forces assaulted the city and Arthur and his men attacked them, fighting far superior numbers. Arthur himself was captured but Merlin saved him. And the Irish were routed when Laodegan's troops joined Arthur's. To reward Arthur, King Laodegan promised him anything he wanted, and since Arthur had fallen in love with his daughter Guinevere, he asked for her hand in marriage. Laodegan not only gave Arthur Guinevere but also a huge oak table of circular shape at which two hundred and fifty knights might be seated. This was the famous Round Table, which was taken to Camelot and became the center of Logres.

Logres was the Arthurian realm of virtue. Any knight who wished to join Arthur's court had to take a vow of virtue. In addition to having courage and might, the chivalric code of Logres required that a knight act honorably, protect the helpless and behave justly to all. Thus Logres was the spiritual counterpart ot Arthur's material kingdom, Britain. It generated enough goodness and bravery to see Arthur and his knights through innumerable times of peril. Britain and Logres were only vulnerable from within, through dissent and treachery in Arthur's court. No external force alone could crush Camelot.

Arthur's most vicious enemy was his half sister, Morgan le Fay. A skilled enchantress, she did everything she could to defeat Arthur. Once Arthur was hunting in Wales with two other knights, Sir Urience and Sir Accolon. They chased a deer until their horses died of exhaustion and the deer fell dead by a large body of water. Extremely tired, the three men saw a ship sail toward them. They embarked and were served by lovely maidens. Soon each fell asleep very deeply. When Arthur awoke he was in a dungeon with other knights. To free the knights he had to fight with a strange knight. When Sir Accolon awoke he was very close to a deep well, and a dwarf told him he must fight a strange knight and gave Sir Accolon Arthur's magic sword and scabbard. Of course this was all the work of Morgan le Fay, who wished to see Arthur slain. The two companions met, fully armed, and Arthur was brutally wounded before he managed to get his own sword back. Neither man would yield even though it meant death. As Arthur was about to kill Accolon he learned he was fighting his own friend and that Morgan le Fay had enchanted each of them. The other hunting companion was Sir Urience, the husband of the sorceress, who awoke in his bed at Camelot beside his wife. In an evil fit Morgan le Fay tried to murder her husband, but a gallant knight prevented her. Fearful that Arthur would take revenge, she stole forth to meet him, and as he lay sleeping she took his scabbard which had rendered him invulnerable. After that she could never return to Camelot. But as a parting gift she sent Arthur a beautiful robe. Suspicious, Arthur had the maiden who brought it try it on first and the maiden was consumed by fire.

GAWAIN

One of the bravest, noblest, and strongest of Arthur's knights was Sir Gawain, but he also had a rash temper. While on his first quest he accidentally killed a lady who was begging for the life of her churlish lover. He did it in pique after the man had pleaded for mercy, and the dishonor affected Gawain deeply. To redeem himself he undertook a dangerous adventure.

A gigantic, awful looking knight, completely green and on a green horse, rode into Camelot brandishing a huge axe. He challenged everyone to strike him a blow with the axe, but whoever did so must take a blow from him a year and a day later in a remote part of Wales at the Green Chapel. Besides Arthur only Gawain was brave enough to accept the challenge. Gawain took the axe and cut off the Green Knight's head at one stroke, whereupon the Green Knight reached over, picked up his head by the green hair, and rode off after reminding Gawain to meet him in a year.

The time came for Gawain to set forth in search of the Green Knight. Knowing that death awaited him, he still intended to fulfill his promise. Gawain asked everywhere for the Green Chapel, to no avail, and journeyed through a forest full of brigands. A week before he was due he came to a castle where he was warmly received by the host and hostess. After staying four days he told the host of his quest and learned that the Green Chapel was but two hours away. The host, a tall, swarthy man, invited Gawain to remain three more days to rest from the hardships of his travels. The host also proposed a game. Gawain would give the host whatever he received in the castle in return for what the host brought back from hunting. Gawain agreed to this.

The next morning the beautiful hostess came to his bed and tried to seduce him, but Gawain merely accepted a kiss from her. When her husband returned with several deer Gawain kissed him to fulfill the bargain. The following day the wife again attempted to seduce Gawain, but he just took two kisses, which he gave to the host returning with a boar's head. On the last day the wife tried every blandishment. Then, seeing she had failed, the wife gave Gawain three kisses and a piece of green lace from her girdle that she said would save his life. However, she told him not to tell her husband. And when the host came home Gawain gave him three kisses for a fox skin.

At last the time had come for Gawain to meet the Green Knight, so he took leave of the host and hostess and rode to the Green Chapel, where he expected to die. There was the terrible Green Knight sharpening his axe for the kill. Gawain submitted, but he flinched as the Green Knight swung at him, for which he was sternly reprimanded. The Green Knight again attempted to cut off Gawain's head, yet he held off at the last instant. On his third try the Green Knight nicked Gawain in the neck, which brought forth blood. At this Gawain sprang up and challenged his adversary, but the Green Knight grew mild and told Gawain of all that had happened with the hostess, including Gawain's taking the green lace to save his own life. Gawain felt he himself should die for such cowardice, and he recognized the Green Knight as his host. Yet the Green Knight hailed Gawain as the bravest knight alive. The Lady of the Lake had cast a spell on the Green Knight to test the value of King Arthur's realm of Logres.

LAUNCELOT

The best knight of Logres was Launcelot of the Lake, who was invincible in combat. Educated by the Lady of the Lake in her underwater castle, Launcelot arrived at the court of King Arthur when he was eighteen. The king and queen immediately recognized him as the peerless knight of whom Merlin had spoken. Launcelot and Guinevere fell instantly in love with each other, and while that love would stir Launcelot to deeds of supreme prowess, it also would result in the downfall of Logres.

Sir Launcelot rode forth to seek adventures with Sir Lionel, but sleepiness overtook him and he dozed off under a tree. Lionel saw a huge knight defeat three other knights. Thinking to win glory he challenged the victor, was beaten in combat, and thrown into a dungeon with other knights. Four queens passed Launcelot as he slept, one of whom was Morgan le Fay. The queens kidnaped the sleeping hero, taking him to a castle where they told him he must choose one of them as a lover or languish in prison. Faithful to Guinevere, Launcelot chose prison, but he was rescued by a young lady who asked him to aid her father in a tournament. Launcelot agreed to help and roundly vanquished her father's opponents. Then he went looking for the huge knight who had taken Sir Lionel prisoner. He challenged the mighty knight and after a fierce contest he slew him, and sent a companion to release Lionel and other knights of Arthur's from their cell. During the night he rescued Sir Kay from three attackers, forcing them to yield to Sir Kay. A lady asked him to rescue a falcon that had become entangled in a tree, and while Launcelot was defenseless in the tree the lady's husband rode up and tried to kill him. However, Launcelot slew the coward with a tree limb. Finally, on this first quest, Launcelot wore Sir Kay's armor home to Camelot and was assaulted by four of Arthur's knights, whom he defeated. When he reached Camelot everyone was hailing him as the greatest knight in the kingdom because of his fine deeds.

Sir Meleagans wished to have Queen Guinevere for himself, and with eighty men he took her and several knights prisoner during a picnic. She sent word to Launcelot to rescue her from Meleagans, but Meleagans arranged an ambush for the knight that left him horseless. After riding in a wood cart, being ridiculed by friends and strangers, being tempted sexually, assaulted by ruffians, magically imprisoned, and set upon by savage beasts, Launcelot arrived at Meleagans' castle. He challenged the lustful knight even though he was weak and exhausted from his many trials. Sir Meleagans might have won the fight if Queen Guinevere had not insulted Launcelot about being unfit to serve her. The remark so angered Launcelot that he killed Meleagans on the spot and restored Guinevere's faith in him.

For many years the love between Launcelot and Guinevere was noble and chaste, but Launcelot was tricked into sin by an enchantment. After rescuing the Dolorous Lady from an evil spell and killing a monstrous dragon, Launcelot came to the Waste Lands and the castle of Carbonek, where King Pelles reigned. Years earlier Sir Balyn, one of Arthur's knights, had come to Carbonek and wounded Pelles with a mystic sword, and Pelles had never healed. A curse had fallen on the land as well, and only the holiest of Arthur's knights could remove the curse, heal King Pelles, or gain the Holy Grail. Launcelot was shown the Grail procession in which three maidens carried the sacred relics of Christ's Passion—the Grail, the platter, and the spear.

In any case King Pelles had a daughter Elaine, and she fell in love with Launcelot, who was pledged to Guinevere. Despairing of winning his love, Elaine went to a sorceress who changed her appearance to that of Guinevere. In this guise Elaine seduced Launcelot and conceived a child by him. When Launcelot learned of the deception, the blot on his honor was so great that he went mad and became a hermit. King Arthur sent many knights out in search of him when he failed to come back, and

Guinevere spent a fabulous sum on the search. Sir Bors rode to Carbonek, where he found Elaine with Sir Launcelot's infant son, Galahad. She told him of all that had happened, and the search continued.

A few years passed and a hermit came again to Elaine's home. It was the mad Launcelot, haggard and exhausted. The holy hermit Naciens took the sleeping knight to a chapel and prayed for him while Sir Bors and Sir Percivale watched and prayed. The Grail magically appeared and disappeared over the altar, and when Launcelot awoke he was sane. However, he needed Elaine's nursing to recover from his hardships as a hermit, yet when he was well he parted from Elaine without giving her a second thought. Later a black barge was found floating down the river to Camelot, and in it was the dead Elaine. She had died for Launcelot's love and was honorably buried. Her son Galahad was reared by monks, and he became the holy knight who would achieve the Sacred Grail for Logres.

GERAINT

One Easter a young man named Geraint came to Arthur's court and announced that he had seen a handsome white stag with golden horns. King Arthur decided to hunt the stag, have Guinevere take Geraint along as a squire, and present Geraint with the stag's head as a trophy for his lady. On the hunt Guinevere saw a gigantic knight accompanied by a lady and a dwarf, so she sent her maid to learn who the strange knight was. The dwarf struck the maid across the face with his whip, and insolently struck Geraint as well when he came to learn the knight's identity. Geraint thought of killing the dwarf but decided against it, since the huge knight was so close. Geraint instead chose to wait until he obtained armor, a spear, and a sword before attacking the knight. Guinevere promised him a knightship at the Round Table if he succeeded.

The young man followed the monstrous knight, lady, and dwarf to a forbidding castle in an unfriendly town. Geraint found only one friendly person in the town, an old man who took him home and introduced him to his wife and his lovely daughter Enid. The old man was formerly the lord of the castle but the knight had usurped it. Geraint said he would fight the knight, and the old man offered him his rusty armor, spear, and shield to fight Yder, the huge knight, on the next day when Yder held his annual tournament. The prize was a silver sparrow hawk to be given to the victor's lady. Since Geraint had no lady, he chose Enid to ride with him. After a hard fight Geraint made Yder yield, so Geraint sent him to Arthur's court to beg Guinevere's pardon for the dwarf's insults. But when Enid learned that Geraint intended to seek further adventure instead of wedding her promptly, she hurt Geraint to the quick with a bitter remark. Angry, Geraint told her to ride in front of him and keep silent.

Enid heard three thieves about to attack them both, but Geraint warned her to keep quiet and killed the thieves, driving them on their horses before him. Then six robbers assaulted Geraint and again he killed them, adding to his spoils. A third time nine brigands attacked, with Geraint warning Enid to remain silent and then killing the nine thieves. The hero now had eighteen suits of armor tied to eighteen horses in a pack before him and Enid. They came to the castle of Sir Oringle, where Geraint still sulked because of Enid's insult. Oringle became enamored of Enid and threatened to kill Geraint on the spot, but Enid said secretly that she would surrender herself on the next day as they rode away. Starting on their journey Enid warned Geraint of their danger, and soon they were accosted by Oringle and a host of knights. Geraint killed many of them, but they overpowered him and rendered him practically dead. Oringle took Enid back to his castle, where she refused to eat or drink until Geraint did so too, for Geraint lay lifeless in the hall. Enraged by her obstinacy, Oringle struck Enid, and her scream brought Geraint out of his coma to cut off Oringle's head. Thinking Geraint a ghost, the others fled from the hall, which allowed Geraint and Enid to escape.

At length the two of them came in sight of King Arthur's hunting party. Sir Kay thought to challenge the strange knight, but Geraint knocked him from his horse. King Arthur and Guinevere hailed Geraint, presenting him with the stag's head, which Geraint gave to Enid. When all of his exploits became known Geraint was duly made a knight of the Round Table.

TRISTRAM

Born of sorrow by a dying woman, Tristram of Lyonesse was raised by foster parents but learned the gentlemanly arts of hunting, minstrelsy, riding, fighting, and languages. Temporarily kidnaped by sailors, he arrived at the court of King Mark of Cornwall, where he distinguished himself in every way. When Marhault of Ireland demanded tribute of King Mark, Tristram challenged the mighty knight. In the fight Marhault received fatal wounds, but he sailed back to Ireland to die. Tristram himself was badly wounded and would not heal, so he sailed off to find a physician. A storm took him to Ireland, where he assumed a false name and went to the Irish court as a minstrel. In return for teaching her daughter, Iseult the Fair, to play the harp Queen Isaud healed Tristram of his wounds.

Back in Cornwall, Tristram told King Mark of the beautiful Iseult, and the king decided to make her his queen. King Mark sent Tristram to Ireland to fetch her. To redeem himself with the Irish for killing Marhault, Tristram slew a dragon that was devastating the land, but another man claimed the credit when Tristram passed out from the dragon's poison. However, it was proved that Tristram had done it, and Queen Isaud forgave him for the death of Marhault. After defeating a knight in combat Tristram was allowed to take Iseult to Cornwall to marry King Mark. And on the voyage Tristram and Iseult unwittingly drank a love potion that caused them to fall deeply and permanently in love.

Yet Iseult was pledged to King Mark, and out of honor she married him. However, she and Tristram held secret meetings together, and a jealous courtier exposed them both to King Mark, who tried to kill Tristram. Instead, Tristram was banished from Cornwall, but he and Iseult still managed to communicate by various means and to hold infrequent rendezvous. Tristram became famous for his knightly services at King Arthur's court, defeating every opponent but Launcelot. He was awarded a seat at the Round Table, but despite his fine exploits he grieved for Iseult's love.

As a consolation he married another woman named Iseult—Iseult of the White Hands. Tristram behaved nobly toward his wife but could not forget his one true love. In trying to save his brother-in-law, Tristram was wounded by a poisoned spear, and he knew that only Iseult the Fair could heal him. He sent a man by ship to bring her, and if she came the sail was to be white, but otherwise a black sail would be hoisted. Too weak to look out the window, Tristram asked his wife to tell him the color of the sail on the approaching ship. It was white, but in a fit of bitter jealousy she told him it was black, and Tristram died. Heartsick at her lover's death, Iseult the Fair also died. Their bodies were taken to King Mark, who forgave them and allowed them to be buried in his own chapel. A vine grew out of Tristram's grave into Iseult's and could not be stopped.

PERCIVALE

After King Pellinore and two of his sons had been slain, his wife took the only remaining son into the seclusion of a deep forest. There Percivale grew up wild, becoming an expert with the dart. When he was fifteen he saw five knights who told him of King Arthur's realm of Logres. Percivale took leave of his mother and rode to Caerleon. As he left the forest he came upon a silken tent in which he found a sleeping maiden. He exchanged rings with her and kissed her mouth as she slept. Then he continued to Caerleon, where Arthur held court.

Upon entering Arthur's hall he found a huge knight in golden armor. The knight rudely took Arthur's drinking cup from the king, drained it, and rode off with it. Arthur said he wanted some lowly fellow to retrieve the cup and avenge the insult. Percivale offered his services, at which Sir Kay took umbrage. And when a maiden addressed the young bumpkin as the finest knight in the realm Sir Kay struck her in the face, for which Percivale vowed revenge. Percivale followed the Red Knight into the country and there he challenged the thief, who attacked. Dodging the thrust of the lance, Percivale killed him as he charged again. Having trouble stripping the Red Knight of his golden armor, Percivale was assisted by Sir Gonemans, an old knight who offered to teach him the arts and code of chivalry.

Percivale spent the summer with Sir Gonemans and then went in search of adventure. He came to the Waste Lands and found the castle of Carbonek, which seemed desolate and empty. He entered and played chess three times on a magic chessboard. He lost each time and drew his sword to hack the mysterious chess pieces to bits, but a maiden rushed up and warned him not to. It was Blanchefleur, the same girl he had kissed in the silken tent. They both confessed their undying love for each other. A clap of thunder filled the castle and three maidens bearing the holy relics of Christ's Passion appeared and then vanished, and Percivale was filled with a sublime peace. Blanchefleur told of the Grail Quest approaching, but Percivale in his enthusiasm for such a quest madly rushed off into the forest, only to find that Carbonek and his true love had disappeared. Sadly he searched for them but he was not destined to find them until the completion of the Grail Quest.

As he rode to Caerleon, Percivale fell rapt in revery. King Arthur and three knights saw the strange knight, and Arthur sent Sir Kay to find out who it was. Percivale did not answer Sir Kay, so Kay struck him with an iron gauntlet, which roused Percivale to fury. Sir Kay was badly wounded in combat and was thereby repaid for his extreme rudeness. Arthur revealed himself, accepted the goblet that the Red Knight had stolen, and then knighted Percivale, telling him that Merlin had foretold his coming. Percivale would arrive at Arthur's court just before the Grail Quest would begin.

THE GRAIL QUEST

The culmination of Arthur's reign and of Logres was the Quest for the Holy Grail, the cup that Christ had used at the Last Supper. Gawain brought back news to Camelot that Merlin had said that every knight must embark on the Grail Quest. A sword in a stone, reserved for a holy knight, was found floating on the river by Camelot. At Pentecost Sir Launcelot made his long-lost son, Galahad, a knight. And the holy hermit, Naciens, introduced Galahad to Arthur's court, where Galahad took his place in the Siege Perilous, a seat that only a saintly knight could occupy. Galahad alone was able to withdraw the sword from the stone, and with it he defeated several knights in tournament. At the Feast of Pentecost every place at the Round Table was occupied at last, and the Grail appeared and vanished in a wondrous way. Gawain vowed to seek the Grail, and every other knight did the same. Arthur was grieved to think that this would be the last time all his knights would gather, for many would die on the Quest. And when the Quest was over, Arthur knew, the end of Logres was near.

Sir Galahad won a shield from a nameless White Knight, a white shield with a cross of blood upon it. He also won a blessing from a hermit knight. Others who had tried to gain them were sorely hurt. At length Galahad was taken aboard the Enchanted Ship that had brought Joseph of Arimathea to England. Sir Percivale had to overcome three manifestations of the devil before he could enter the Enchanted Ship; first as an unruly black stallion that nearly carried him off, then as a serpent that was strangling a lion, and finally as a lovely seductress. He was saved only by calling on the power of Heaven. Sir Bors de Gannis was allowed upon the Enchanted Ship as well after rescuing a lady from a rapist, resisting the lady's seductions, and submitting to the cruelty of his maddened elder brother. Last, Sir Launcelot came aboard the Enchanted Ship once he had confessed his sinful love for Queen Guinevere and done penance for it. Each of these knights was led aboard the Enchanted Ship by Dindrane, the sister of Percivale and a nun.

The Enchanted Ship sailed along and put into a bay, where the four knights and the nun disembarked. Outside a castle they were attacked by a company of knights, but they defended themselves well. Then a Golden Knight rode up, the lord of the castle, and he called off his men. The Golden Knight had an ailing wife who could only be healed by a virgin's blood. Many maidens had died in giving impure blood, but Dindrane offered her own blood, which healed the lady but caused Dindrane to die. The castle itself was then burnt to charred ruins because of the evil that had been done there. Sir Bors rode on with Sir Galahad toward the Waste Lands, while Sir Percivale and Sir Launcelot pursued further adventures.

Sir Gawain met Sir Ector while riding in the Waste Lands and they exchanged gossip about what others had done on the Quest. The two came to a deserted chapel. That night a mysterious voice warned Sir Ector to quit the Quest, which he did. Sir Gawain, however, saw a mysterious candlestick lighted and extinguished. In the morning Naciens the hermit told him that he had the power to lift the curse from the Waste Lands if he kept himself pure. Gawain rode on and encountered Sir Launcelot, and both of them came to the castle of Carbonek, where they were greeted by King Pelles. A feast of rich food and wine was set before the two knights. Sir Launcelot ate of it and fell asleep, but Sir Gawain ate only bread and water and kept silent despite the taunts of others present. A clap of thunder announced the Grail procession of the three maidens carrying the holy relics. Gawain got up and asked the Grail Maiden what these things meant. He was told to follow, and he did so. Sir Launcelot tried to follow too but was only permitted a glimpse of the Grail, at which he fell in a swoon, whereas Gawain was allowed a full vision of the mystic cup. He had lifted the curse from the Waste Lands, but the full completion of the Grail Quest was for others.

Sir Percivale caught up with Sir Bors and Sir Galahad as they rode to Carbonek. The three knights were greeted by Pelles and Naciens in the castle. They declined the rich fare, eating merely bread and water. Again at the peal of thunder the Grail procession of three maidens appeared, and a sacred ritual took place in which Sir Galahad drank from the Holy Grail, relieved Naciens the monk of the ancient curse that Joseph of Arimathea had laid upon him, and healed King Pelles of the wound that had afflicted him for years. Sir Percivale recognized the Grail Maiden as his true love Blanchefleur, who had vanished. After piecing a mystic sword together, Percivale married Blanchefleur under Galahad's supervision, and he became King of Carbonek when Pelles died. His mission accomplished, Sir Galahad was transfigured before the court, and he died. Sir Bors rode back to Camelot to tell of the completion of the Grail Quest and of the hour in which the glory of Logres was fulfilled.

THE PASSING OF ARTHUR'S REALM

Several seats at the Round Table now were empty, and Arthur knew that Logres would soon succumb to the forces of darkness as Merlin had prophesied. Sir Launcelot was the ablest knight in the kingdom, but he sinned adulterously with Queen Guinevere, and through that sinning he brought about a fatal breach in Arthur's court. Sir Modred was Arthur's bastard son by Morgause, the wife of King Lot. Modred was envious of Arthur's power, so he conspired with Gawain's brother Agravain to cause strife between Arthur and Launcelot. The two conspirators overheard Guinevere invite Launcelot secretly to her room one night. They told King Arthur, who empowered them to take twelve knights and surprise the loving couple together, which they did. Sir Launcelot was defenseless, but he killed an attacker and put on the man's armor. Then he killed Agravain, wounded Modred, and made his escape.

Modred went again to Arthur and told him of all that had transpired. He insisted that Guinevere be put to death as an adulteress. Arthur sadly agreed that this was the law. Guinevere was to be burned at the stake. Arthur tried to get Gawain to attend, but he refused and sent two more of his brothers instead. As the pyre was being lighted Sir Launcelot rode up with a company of knights, killed many of Arthur's men, including Gawain's brothers, and rescued the queen from the fire. They retreated to Launcelot's castle, the Joyous Gard, and Arthur and Gawain laid siege to the place. Whenever Arthur was tempted to make peace with Launcelot, Gawain grew angry, for he was carrying on a blood feud with Launcelot. At last Launcelot in a spirit of generosity saved Arthur's life during a battle, and when he offered to return Guinevere and exile himself from England Arthur made truce with him. So Launcelot went to Armorica in France.

However, Gawain wanted Launcelot's life, so he raised an army and persuaded Arthur to attack Launcelot in France. The Saxons, having learned of the civil war, began invading England once more. And in Arthur's absence Sir Modred announced that Arthur had died in France and persuaded the people to elect himself king, after which he was crowned at Canterbury. Modred tried unsuccessfully to take Guinevere as his queen. On threatening the Archbishop, Modred was excommunicated. When Arthur learned of what was happening in his own realm he withdrew from France to return to Dover, where he and his army were met by Modred's forces. In the fighting Modred and his troops were routed. Gawain, who had received terrible wounds from Launcelot in France, was wounded again fatally at Dover. Yet on his deathbed he wrote Launcelot, begging his forgiveness and urging him to return to Britain to save Arthur's kingdom from Modred.

Within a short time Modred had gathered an army of a hundred thousand men and was harassing western Britain. Arthur took his army to Camlann to meet Modred. The night before the battle Gawain appeared to Arthur in a vision and told him to make a truce with Modred for a month, until Launcelot could come to his aid. So Arthur made a truce with Modred as the two armies confronted one another. Yet when a soldier drew his sword to kill a snake that had stung him the two forces charged one another. By evening both armies were almost completely annihilated. On Arthur's side only Arthur and two knights, both badly hurt, were left alive. Arthur suddenly saw Modred and in a fury the two men assaulted each other. Modred was slain outright, while Arthur was fatally hurt. He told his two remaining knights to carry him to a nearby lake, and one of them died while lifting him. Arthur then told the other to throw his sword Excalibur into the lake. The knight was reluctant to do so, but on Arthur's insistence he did it and a hand reached out of the lake and seized the sword. Then a barge came sailing up with the Lady of the Lake, the Lady of Avalon, and Morgan le Fay. They took Arthur aboard and sailed to the Isle of Avalon, where Arthur would rest until Britain would need him again.

Sir Launcelot returned to Britain to find the realm of Logres completely extinguished. Gawain and Arthur were dead, along with every knight of the Round Table but five. Guinevere had become a nun to repent of the sin that had destroyed Logres, and Launcelot followed her example by becoming a monk. When those two died the four knights remaining undertook a pilgrimage to the Holy Land. And England was overrun with barbarians

Commentary

These legends are strongly medieval in flavor. Magic enchantments and miracles abound, yet despite the fantastic elements there is a hard basis of reality underlying these tales. Not a factual reality, but the kind that fiction presents. The world here is coherent: it makes sense. King Arthur is the center of that world, and by his valor, his strength, and his high purpose he collects an assembly of knights who share his purpose. These knights vie with one another to test their courage, might, and nobility. They undergo temptations that they must resist if they are to perform great deeds. Above all, they must be unselfish, for they are serving a power greater than themselves, the ideal of Logres, the holy realm. Logres is a place where faith works miracles and where the power of Heaven supports the weak and the humble. Frequently in these stories a knight fails to live up to this communal ideal, but he must pay for it in the end. Arthur begets Modred on his half sister adulterously, and Modred is the agent of Arthur's ruin. Launcelot and Guinevere destroy Logres with their love affair. And Tristram through his love for King Mark's wife endures exile and death.

There seems to be a general logic to the magic spells and miracles of these tales. Enchantments are used to test the knights of the Round Table. When another person suffers from a spell it takes a knight to redeem that person. When a knight undergoes enchantment it is to test his integrity. To witness a miracle a knight must have passed his tests of character. Thus wonders in these tales are not just the furnishings of an age of faith, for they serve to reveal a man's character.

This is our first example of a band of heroes fighting for abstract principles of justice, honor, and purity. These knights have serious flaws—pride, lust, rashness, vengefulness—but they rise above their faults in the contribution they make to Logres. Each knight is tested for his weaknesses. Only the holiest of knights, Sir Galahad, is allowed to drink from the Holy Grail. The Grail Quest is the summation of Logres, the period when each knight sets forth on an unselfish mission.

These assorted tales carry an extremely important insight-that a man's self-respect does not depend on external qualities, such as wealth, position, physical strength, or size. It depends on his private integrity and his valor in pursuing great goals. This is the kind of insight that builds civilizations.

Bibliographical Essay

Our knowledge of the mythologies related here derives from literary works chiefly—from epic and lyric poetry, from drama, histories, romances, and from other prose narratives. But it is important to distinguish between mythology, which is religious and social belief rendered in stories, and the literary form those stories take. Literature is often a late product of civilizations. It occurs when there is enough leisure to record and invent tales, and enough literacy to appreciate the records. Because it usually occurs late in a culture, mythological writing sometimes takes place as a culture is disintegrating. When doubt becomes wide-spread it is doubly necessary to record a people's myths—to preserve them from extinction and to form a core from which other cultures can be built. When root values are endangered people take care to preserve them in stories. Mythological literature may be seen in part as an embalming of a culture, the point where a living faith is becoming a historical curiosity. This is not always true of course (the Bible being a notable exception), but it holds often enough in the mythologies recounted here.

In Egyptian myth there is a bewildering profusion of gods and sacred names. The pyramid texts refer to several myths without telling them in their entirety. We must rely on a foreigner, Plutarch, the late Greek historian, for a complete account of the Isis and Osiris myth. This tale points to a static, worshipful culture, one founded on moral struggle, death, and an afterlife to come.

The principal Babylonian mythological works are the *Epic of Creation* and the *Gilgamesh Epic,* which reveal a rather coarsely masculine culture, sensual and proud, yet with a deep pessimism in the face of death.

Indian mythology is vast, scattered through many literary works: The *Vedas,* the *Brahmanas,* the *Upanishads,* the *Mahabharata,* the *Ramayama,* and Buddhist writings, to name some of them. They show a culture evolving from a primitive worship of nature and earthly power to metaphysical speculation and a realization of saintly principles.

In its literary manifestations Classical mythology covers over a thousand years of writing. It starts with Homer, who lived about 800 B.C. and remains the greatest epic poet of the West; and it ends with the Roman elegiac poet Musaeus, a minor writer who lived in the fifth century A.D.. It includes some of the world's best writing and some of its dullest. Moreover, it includes two very distinct cultures, the Greek and the Roman.

Greek mythology is colorful, individualistic, amazingly diversified, and rationalistic. It displays a culture where personal honor is paramount and in which conflict is always present. Homer is both ebullient and stark in the way he depicts war. He delights in his senses, in courage and prowess, but he also shows the horrors of death. He is casual toward the gods, admiring their might but laughing at their human antics. Opposed to him is the early poet Hesiod, fierce, pious, a bit naive, but full of powerful conviction in the gods. He dislikes Homer's irreverent attitude. However, Homer's *Iliad* and *Odyssey* and Hesiod's *Theogony* contribute much to our knowledge of Greek myths.

The *Homeric Hymns,* recorded from 700 B.C. to about 450 B.C., were poems in praise of various gods that told of their various exploits. Pindar, a lyrical poet of the late sixth century B.C., wrote *Odes* celebrating the winners of Greek festivals in which myths were referred to or explicitly told. Pindar was as pious as Hesiod, but he expurgated the brutal elements and rationalized the myths for a more sophisticated audience.

The Greek dramatists, Aeschylus, Sophocles, Euripides, and Aristophanes, used myths as material for their dramas. Aeschylus explored the problem of divine justice, Sophocles employed myth to delve into innocent suffering and retribution; and Euripides used myth to present divine injustices. Aristophanes, however, referred to myths in a casual manner. In about a century, from around 500 B.C. to 400 B.C., Greek drama reflected a devolution from high faith to profound disillusionment.

Prose writers such as the historian Herodotus and the philosopher Plato wrote on mythological material, and Plato in fact created philosophical parables in a mythical vein. But after Plato and Aristotle Athenian culture was bankrupt, and a new Greek culture arose in Alexandria in Egypt. It was softer, sadder, and somewhat effete. Apollonius of Rhodes wrote his *Argonautica,* the story of Jason, and the Alexandrian poets turned to love and pastoral subjects as principal themes.

Then the Romans took over, a tough, unimaginative people to whom mythology was essentially foreign. They worshiped the State and the family to whom their gods were subservient. The Romans borrowed myths from Greek civilization but had few of their own. The myths they had were usually historical legends involving political heroes. Yet they made a contribution to literature in a mythological vein, largely through the historian Livy and the poet Vergil. Other writers, too, took up mythological material. Ovid was fascinated by love and female psychology. His *Metamorphoses, Fasti,* and *Heroides* take up mythological subjects charmingly, but without belief. Apuleius probably invented the myth of Cupid and Psyche. Musaeus wrote of Hero and Leander. This obsession with love and passion was characteristic of decadent Romans. Lucian, who wrote in the second century A.D. satirized the gods. Apollodorus wrote an encyclopedic account of the old myths to preserve them. And Pausanias took a tour of Greece, a sentimental journey in the second century A.D., to visit the sites of mythological occurrences, and wrote of his travels in *Descriptions of Greece.* Roman culture had exhausted itself.

The Teutonic myths of northern Europe, as they were preserved in Tacitus and the Icelandic *Eddas,* show a hard, warlike, gloomy culture in which one's pleasures were few but very intense. The Anglo-Saxon epic of *Beowulf* reveals the noble side of Teutonic ethics.

Arthurian legends were recorded in medieval romances and point to the Christianization of the old warrior code. Chivalry sublimated tribal warfare into combat for abstract principles of justice, purity, and honor. Love, often adulterous love, provided a pretext for valorous deeds in the romances. From the early Welsh tales recorded in *The Mabinogeon* to Malory's *Morte d'Arthur* in the fifteenth century, the tales of Arthur and his knights grew in richness and depth. But by the time of Malory the knightly armored cavalry was almost obsolete.

Each culture seems to create a distinct heroic type that is easily recognizable. The goals of a society determine the kind of hero it honors. Our culture is no exception, and like these extinct civilizations we tend to articulate our values when they are threatened. America's great contribution to popular mythology so far has been the cowboy. For over a hundred years the stereotype of the loner cowboy, tough, honorable, resourceful, has been reiterated in the media, just as America was becoming urban, bureaucratized, industrial. Whatever new heroic types emerge from our culture will probably be slightly outmoded, fighting barbarian forces in whatever guise they come.

Review Questions

1. Discuss the differences between pure myth, heroic saga, the folk tale, the romance, and the symbolic tale. Give an example of each type.
2. Why do men give human traits and motives to the gods?
3. Are gods usually personified natural elements, such as fire, water, wind, etc? Or are they beings that manipulate nature?
4. From what cultures do these gods come? Mars, Ishtar, Indra, Gaea, Ra, Thor, Marduk, Set, Vishnu, Odin, Pan, Janus.
5. Give the Latin names of these Greek gods: Cronus, Zeus, Hera, Poseidon, Hades, Demeter, Aphrodite, Hephaestus, Athena, Artemis, Apollo, Ares, Hestia, Hermes, and Per sephone.
6. What does the Greek account of the creation show about the Greek character?
7. Compare the Egyptian, Babylonian, Greek, and Norse accounts of the creation.
8. Explain Zeus's amorousness in terms of Greek values.
9. Account for the individuality and specialization of the Greek gods. What happened to these gods when Rome took them over?
10. Which heroes are associated with the following monsters? Medusa, Grendel, the Harpies, Polyphemus, the Minotaur, the Hydra, Khumbaba, the Chimaera, Fafnir the dragon.
11. Show how the following heroes reflected the values of their respective civilizations: Osiris—Egypt, Gilgamesh—Babylonia, Rama—India, Heracles—Greece, Beowulf—Norse, Launcelot—medieval.
12. Take three Greek heroes and show their differences and similarities. How does their character affect their destiny?
13. Show the different themes that run through the Greek tragic dynasties and indicate their significance. Use the stories as evidence.
14. What unity does the tale of the Trojan War have, if any? Discuss the importance of this tale to the Greeks.

15. Why was conflict so pronounced in Greek myths and culture?
16. How was the patriotic legend valuable to the Romans?
17. Explain the Roman preoccupation with love. Use examples. What does such a preoccupation often indicate about a culture?
18. Discuss the importance of warfare in Norse myth.
19. In Arthurian legend what is Logres? Show how it operated as a communal ideal in Arthur's court.
20. Imagine yourself a thousand years in the future. Write a myth or legend of our era as it might evolve. Take the Kennedy dynasty as an example and treat it in a mythical vein.

Recommended Reading

Primary Sources

AESCHYLUS. *The Complete Greek Tragedies*, vols. I-II. Edited by DAVID GRENE and RICHMOND LATTIMORE. New York, Modern Library.

APULEIUS. *The Golden Ass*. Translated by ROBERT GRAVES. New York: Farrar, Strauss & Giroux, 1951.

Beowulf. Translated by WILLIAM ELLERY LEONARD. New York: Appleton, 1923.

The Elder Edda. Translated by PAUL B. TAYLOR and W. H. AUDEN. London: Faber & Faber, 1969.

The Epic of Gilgamesh. Translated by N. K. SANDERS. Baltimore: Penguin, 1960.

EURIPIDES. *The Complete Greek Tragedies*, vols. V-VII. Edited by DAVID GRENE and RICHMOND LATTIMORE. New York, Modern Library.

GODOLPHIN, F. R. B., ed. *Great Classical Myths*. New York: Modern Library, 1964.

HESIOD. *The Theogony* and *The Works and Days*. Translated by RICHMOND LATTIMORE. Ann Arbor: University of Michigan Press, 1959.

HOMER. *The Iliad of Homer*. Translated by RICHMOND LATTIMORE. Chicago: University of Chicago Press, 1951.

———. *The Odyssey*. Translated by ROBERT FITZGERALD. New York: Doubleday & Co., 1961.

MALORY, SIR THOMAS. *Le Morte d'Arthur*. Translated by KEITH BAINES. New York: Bramhall House, 1962.

OVID. *The Metamorphoses*. Translated by HORACE GREGORY. New York: Mentor, 1960.

PINDAR. *Odes*. Translated by RICHMOND LATTIMORE. Chicago: University of Chicago Press, 1947.

PLUTARCH. *Isis and Osiris*. Translated by F. C. BABBITT. Cambridge, Mass.: Harvard University Press, Loeb Classical Library, 1936.

SOPHOCLES. *The Complete Greek Tragedies*, vols. III-IV. Edited by DAVID GRENE and RICHMOND LATTIMORE. New York, Modern Library.

VERGIL. *The Aeneid*. Translated by PATRICK DICKINSON. New York: Mentor, 1960.

Secondary Sources

BOWRA, C. M. *The Greek Experience*. New York: Mentor, 1959. Excellent account of Greek culture.

BULFINCH, THOMAS. *Bulfinch's Mythology*. New York, Modern Library. Standard version of Classical and Arthurian myths and legends.

EVANS, BERGEN. *Dictionary of Mythology*. Lincoln, Nebr.: Centennial Press, 1970. A fine, witty reference work.

GOODRICH, NORMA LORRE. *Ancient Myths*. New York: Mentor, 1960. Lively retelling of myths of many cultures.

______. *The Medieval Myths*. New York: Mentor, 1961. Excellent retellings of assorted medieval myths.

GRANT, MICHAEL. *Myths of the Greeks and Romans*. New York: Mentor, 1964. First-rate scholarship, well written.

GRAVES, ROBERT. *The Greek Myths*. 2 vols. Baltimore: Penguin, 1955. Vivid renderings of the myths, very informative.

HAMILTON, EDITH. *Mythology*. New York: Mentor, 1942. Excellent retelling of Classical and Norse myths.

Larousse Encyclopedia of Mythology. Introduction by ROBERT GRAVES. New York: Prometheus Press, 1968. Good, scholarly survey of the world's mythologies. Lavishly illustrated.

LOOMIS, R. S. *Arthurian Literature in the Middle Ages*. Oxford: Clarenden Press, 1959. Fine study.

ROSE, H. J. *A Handbook of Greek Mythology*. London: Methuen, 1959. Scholarly account of Greek and Roman myths.

SEYFERT, OSKAR. *A Dictionary of Classical Antiquities*. Revised and edited by HENRY NETTLESHIP and J. E. SANDYS. New York: Meridian, 1956. Fine reference work.

ZIMMERMAN, J. E. *Dictionary of Classical Mythology*. New York: Bantam, 1964. Useful and detailed.

Genealogical Tables

THE IMPORTANT GREEK GODS (Olympian Gods Capitalized)

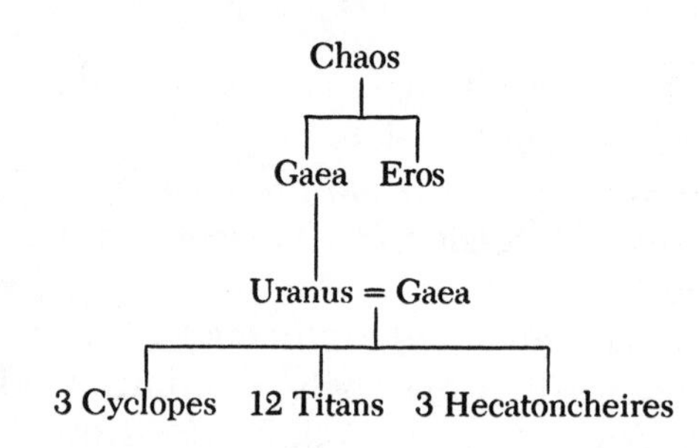

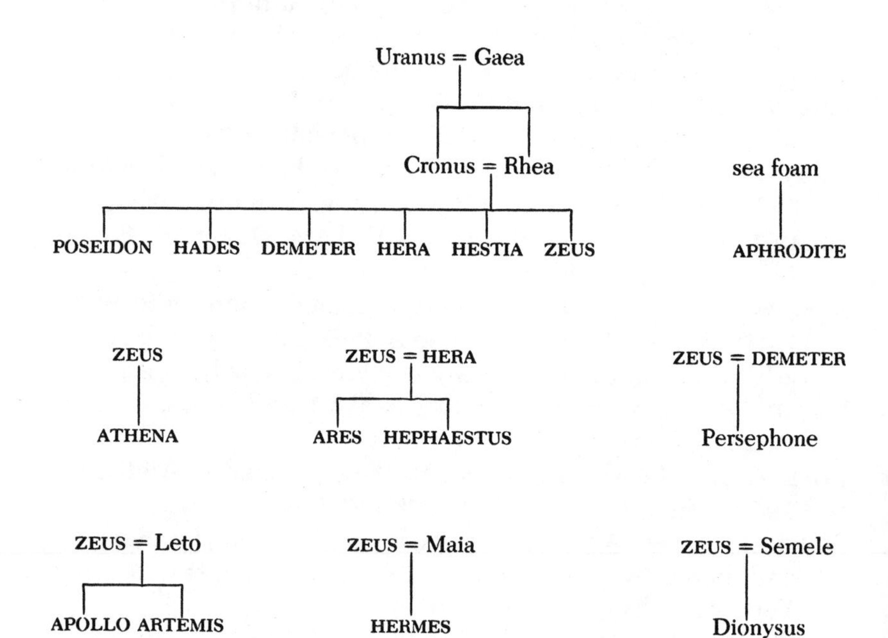

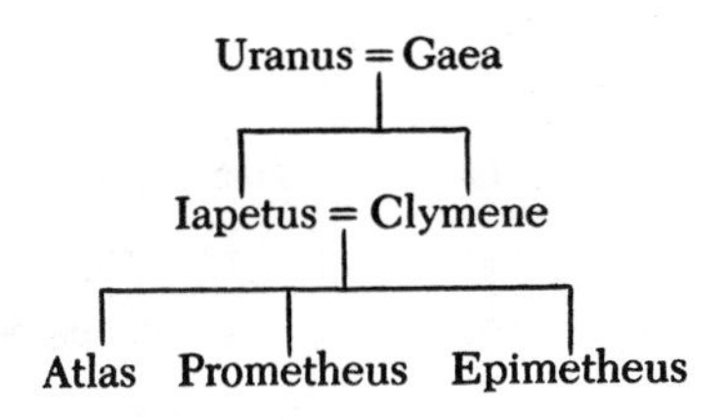

THE GREEK TRAGIC DYNASTIES

Minos of Crete

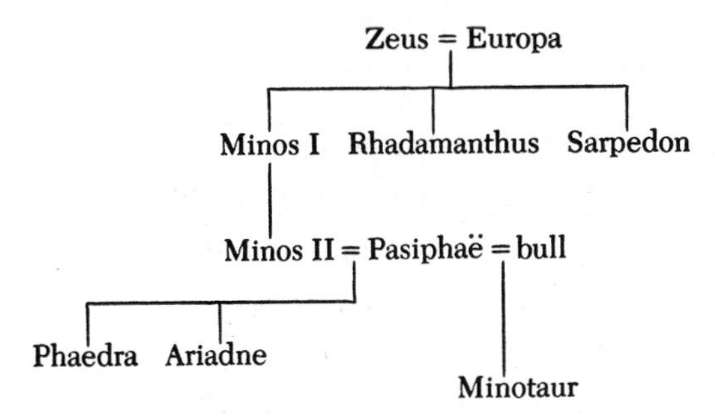

Atreus of Mycenae

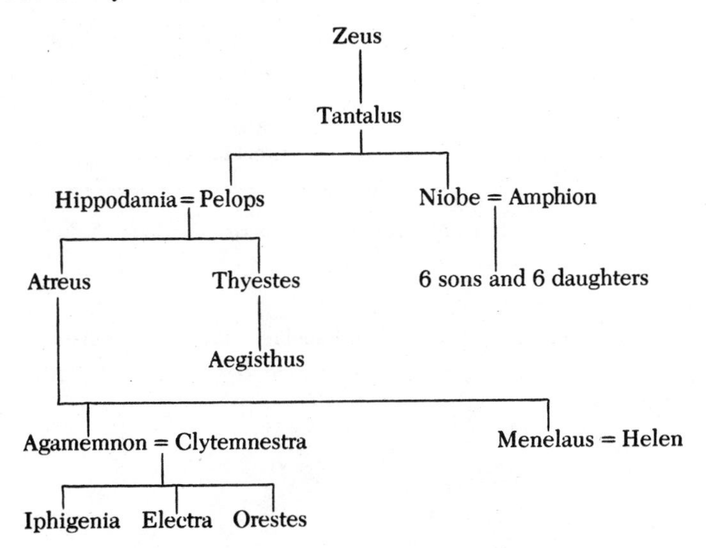

Cadmus of Thebes

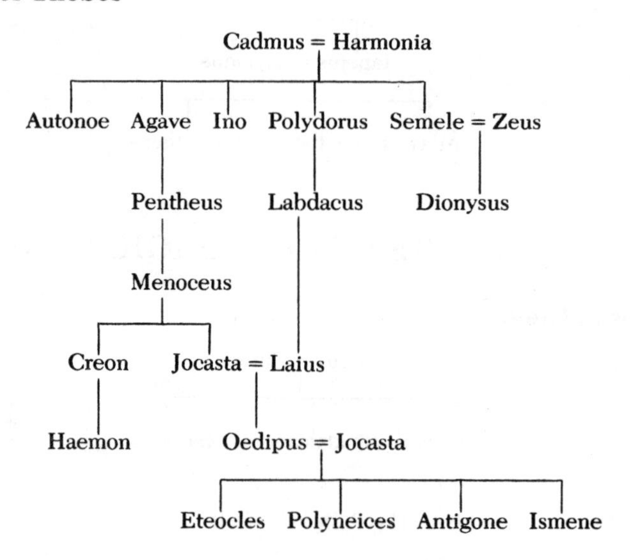

Erichthonius of Athens

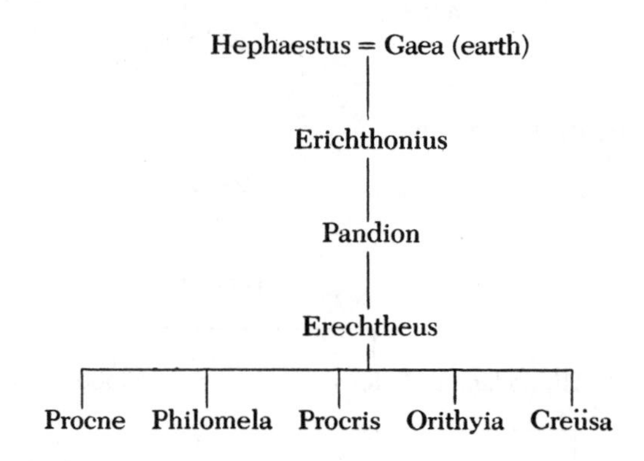

Procne = Tereus = Philomela

Itys

Procris = Cephalus

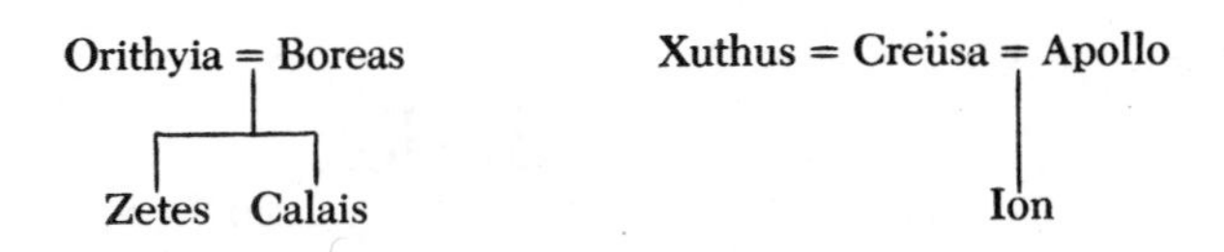

ARTHURIAN GENEALOGIES

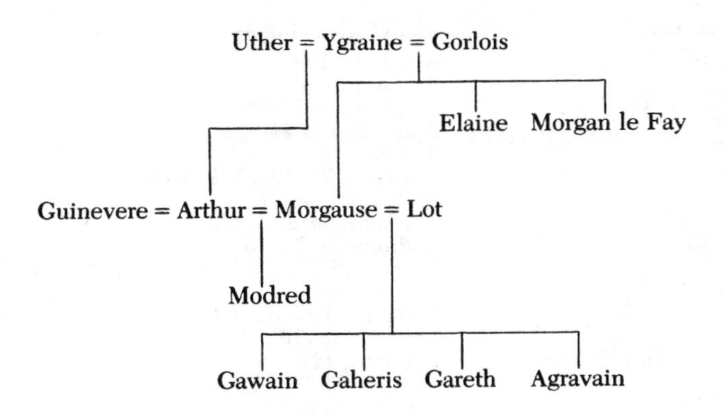

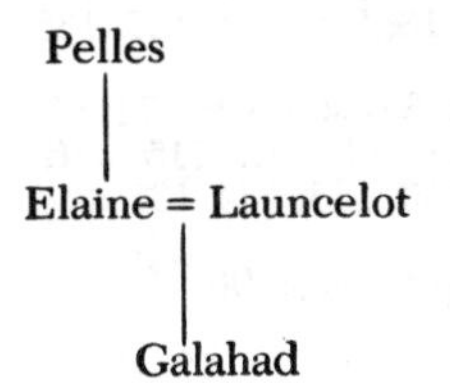

Index